BIRDS *in medieval manuscripts*

BIRDS
in medieval manuscripts

BRUNSDON YAPP

THE BRITISH LIBRARY

Plates © 1981 The British Library Board
Text © 1981 Brunsdon Yapp
ISBN 0 904654 54 0

Published by the British Library
Reference Division Publications
Great Russell Street
London WC1B 3DG

British Library Cataloguing in Publication Data

Yapp, William Brunsdon
    Birds in medieval manuscripts.
1. Illumination of books and manuscripts
I. Title
745.6′7   ND 2920

Designed by Frank Phillips
Set in 12/13pt. Times Roman by Channel 8 Ltd, Bexhill-on-Sea
Figures and plates originated by Culver Graphics Ltd, High Wycombe
Printed and bound in Hong Kong by Mandarin Offset Marketing (H.K.) Ltd

CONTENTS

Preface 6
Introduction 8
   The Birds 12
     Non-passerine birds:
      Cranes and other long-legged birds 13
      Domestic birds 19
      Eagles and vultures 26
      Game-birds and wildfowl 28
      Hawks and falcons 33
      Owls 35
      Parrot 43
      Pigeons 44
      Sea-birds 47
      Waders 50
      Miscellaneous non-passerines 53
     Passerine birds:
      Crows 56
      Finches and similar birds 58
      Swallows 61
      Thrushes 64
      Tits 66
      Miscellaneous passerines 68
   Conclusions 71
Colour plates 80
The references: a note for the reader 176
Bibliography 177
Acknowledgements 181
Index of birds 183
Index of manuscripts 186
General index 189

PREFACE

I hope that this book will interest three classes of reader. First, perhaps, those interested in birds, whether back-garden feeders of tits and robins or professional ornithologists, who will want to know how people looked at birds between five and thirteen hundred years ago; secondly, the general reader willing to learn anything new about the past; lastly, art-historians who will, I hope, find it informative, even if they are surprised by some of my conclusions. It is the first study of the subject on this scale and it follows only very few papers in learned journals. There are a few books on animals in art, but none says much about birds, and all suffer from having been written by authors whose knowledge of the creatures was small, so that misidentifications, sometimes of the crudest sort, abound.

Since a professional worker in medieval manuscripts can write of them 'Many of those in public collections are still unfamiliar even to specialists' (Backhouse 1979), it is obvious that a zoologist like myself, coming to their study only after retirement, must be ignorant of many that he ought to know. I am fairly confident that there are likely to be few

English manuscripts with many birds that I do not know, but whether my sample of continental manuscripts is a fair one is more doubtful; it is certainly much smaller than I should like. I have been restricted to English libraries (and one Scottish) and have seen, for example, only 28 continental Books of Hours, with another 34 in full or partial reproduction in colour, while there are said to be more than 400 in the Bibliothèque Nationale alone. I can only hope that those manuscripts bought by the great English collectors, or selected, for whatever reason, for publication by scholars, are suitable representatives for the discussion of birds.

One other point is important. For critical study there is no substitute for seeing the actual manuscript. Many birds cannot be identified from black and white photographs, and colour plates are sometimes inaccurate — compare, for example, the same folio of Les Grandes Heures du Jean Duc de Berri, in Harthan (1977) Pl. 59 and Thomas (1979) Pl. 20, where golden-brown in one becomes green in the other. I have seen the majority of the manuscripts that I discuss — 154 out of 187 of those mentioned, and all but three of those which are illustrated in colour in this book. These are selected from over 400 manuscripts with birds, more than three-quarters of them English, that I have examined, with another 80, more than three-quarters foreign, that I have seen only in reproduction. While many are well-known to art-historians, others are less familiar, and have seldom or never been reproduced before.

Where practicable, proofs of the colour plates have been compared with the actual manuscripts.

The study on which this book is based could not have been done without the help of many friends and some strangers, or without the co-operation of librarians and their staffs. I am grateful to all, including those in charge of a few libraries whose manuscripts are not mentioned here and of one in which I was somewhat frustrated by not being allowed to turn over the pages. I am especially grateful to His Grace the Duke of Northumberland for twice allowing me to see the Sherborne Missal (perhaps the most beautiful manuscript in England, and certainly the most interesting for its birds) and to Mr. Leslie Brown for assisting my rusty and rudimentary knowledge of Latin.

B.Y.

Church End. May 1981.

INTRODUCTION

The colour plates in this book are taken from 41 manuscripts ranging in date from AD 698 to 1482, by which time printing had been introduced and the inevitable decline in the handwritten and illuminated book had begun. They illustrate 83 species of bird which can be identified with some certainty, while nine more are shown in black and white and four are not illustrated. Some of the 41 manuscripts, as well as others not represented, contain a few species the identity of which can only be guessed at.

Although chosen for their birds, the plates also illustrate many of the different types of illuminated manuscript produced in England and western Europe between the establishment of the Saxon kingdoms and the introduction of printing. Different types of book are characteristic of different periods. Amongst the earliest are copies of the four Gospels, sumptuously decorated both within and without, which were intended for liturgical reading in church. The 11th and 12th centuries are noted for enormous Bibles, also designed for reading in public and certainly requiring a lectern to support their immense weight. The 13th century saw a marked rise in the demand for books for individual use and pocket-sized Bibles became fashionable. Personal psalters, used for private devotions by both clerics and laymen, were amongst the most richly illuminated manuscripts of this century and the next. The Apocalypse (the Book of Revelation) and the Bestiary (a collection of largely mythical information about animals, plants and minerals) also survive in substantial numbers. The most popular book of the later Middle Ages, especially in France, was the Book of Hours, essentially a devotional manual, the main contents of which were services to be said at different hours of the day.

While the pictures of birds in the bestiaries serve, at least when they are accurately drawn, an essential purpose (Pls. 17–18), and those illustrating scenes in the Bible such as the Creation (Pls. 8–10) or the 'Call of the Birds' in the Apocalypse (Pls. 13–16) help in the understanding of the story, in most of the other books they are used merely as decoration, with little or no relevance to the text. This is especially so at the beginning of the period with the Anglo-Celtic Gospels (Pls. 3–5) and at the end with

French Books of Hours (Pls. 42–47). Throughout this time secular books were produced; most of these were unillustrated, but some have pictures of birds that are relevant to the text (Pls. 19–20; Figs. 3,4), while a few, especially in the later Middle Ages, use birds as decoration (Pl. 39).

Except for one or two comparisons, I have said little of the *De arte venandi cum avibus* of Frederick II (Vatican, MS.Pal.Lat. 1071; facsimile, 1969). Its birds deserve a discussion to themselves; they are remarkable for their time (mid-thirteenth century), even though they are not as good representations as has sometimes been claimed, but since they have neither known predecessors nor (except for two French copies) successors, they do not fit easily into any general account of medieval birds. There is no justification for the view that they influenced the artists of English manuscripts of 20 or 30 years later, since their style is completely different.

This book does not consider eastern manuscripts, nor those from Spain. Except at the very end of the period, such Spanish bird illustrations as I have seen are strikingly different from those occurring elsewhere in Europe; the depiction of the 'Call of the Birds' in a Spanish commentary on the Apocalypse of c.1109 (Fig. 1) may be compared with the same scene in English books (Pls. 13–16). Of the 41 manuscripts illustrated in colour 31 or 32 are English. Apocalypses and bestiaries were predominantly English. In the illustration of Bibles there is probably little to choose between continental and English examples

Fig. 1. *Apocalypse, Commentary of Beatus of Liébana; the 'Call of the Birds' (19:17–18).* B.L. MS. Add. 11695, f. 197r. Spanish, 1109. The birds are variously black, yellow and red.

(e.g. Pl. 12). The sudden flourishing of birds as decoration in English Psalters (Pls. 21–30,32–34; Fig. 2) for a few decades before and after 1300 has no parallel elsewhere. It was not until a century later, in the Franco-Flemish Books of Hours (Pls.

Fig. 2. *St. Omer Psalter, B.L. MS. Add. 39810, f. 7r, lower border (detail of Pl. 28). English, c. 1330.*

42–47), that the continent took the lead in the depiction of birds.

The Bestiary or Physiologus probably originated in Greece in the 4th or 5th century, and then included only 13 birds, of which the phoenix certainly and perhaps others were mythical. The Latin versions that circulated in Europe and especially in England in the later Middle Ages apparently all derived from what is known as 'Versio B' (because the main source is a manuscript at Berne), and were divided by James (1928) into four 'families'. His classification has been developed by McCulloch (1962). The first 'family' is subdivided into (i) a group called 'B-Is', because it contains additions from the *Etymologiae* of Isidore of Seville (c.560–636); (ii) another based on the *Aviarium* of Hugh of Folieto, who wrote in the 12th century; and (iii) a 'transitional' group. The greatest number of surviving copies belong to the second 'family', and contain about 30 birds. There are only five known copies of the third 'family', and only one (C.U.L. MS.Gg.6.5) of the fourth, which contains over 50 species. This method of division is based solely on the text; the illustrations have not been fully studied, but a comparison of the birds depicted in 48 bestiaries shows that while there are resemblances within a 'family' there are often also considerable differences. There is unfortunately no easily-accessible account of the 'families', but a useful history of the Bestiary is given by White (1954), which also includes a translation of C.U.L. MS.Ii.4.26, of the second 'family', with its pictures (mostly uncoloured in the original) reproduced in line.

Except for a few fragments there are no English vernacular bestiaries, but there are several French translations, three of them in verse, usually named after their translators (Philippe de Thaon, Gervaise, Guillaume le Clerc (William the Norman), Pierre de Beauvais). These must have come originally from one or more Latin versions, but they developed independently of the 'families', and their illustrations are completely different.

Although the Latin names of the birds in the Bestiary are often the same as the modern scientific ones, they must not be confused with them, and some are different; the bestiary *fulica,* for example, is not the modern coot, which scientists call *Fulica atra.* Bestiary names are italicised in this book, but not given capitals except where they begin a sentence.

THE BIRDS

The following account of the birds is arranged under groups that a medieval naturalist might have recognised; they are only approximately those of a modern classification, being based on ecology and general appearance rather than structure. Non-passerines (roughly, the larger birds of moor and water) come first, in alphabetical order, and then the passerines (the ordinary birds of woodland and garden). The occurence of each group in more than 300 English and 70 continental manuscripts is discussed; these I have examined myself, and I have also taken account of reproductions of manuscripts that I have not seen, especially of those made elsewhere than in England. In addition, the birds of nearly 50 bestiaries that I have examined are, if relevant, dealt with separately. The likely geographical distribution of the birds during the Middle Ages, if it differs from that of the present time, is also noted.

Identification is not always easy. Where a bird has a strong pattern of colour that is well reproduced, as in many pictures of goldfinches, there can be no doubt, but many drawings are inaccurate, and one may suspect careless copying; this is well seen in a series of cranes and parrots in the Bible of William of Devon (B.L. MS.Roy.1.D.i), where some of the birds could hardly be recognised if they could not be compared with other, better, drawings in the series. Some birds have few striking characters and in such cases one may not be able, in the absence of precise detail, to decide which species the artist intended to represent. Sometimes, however, he did notice and show such small features as the red splash on the bill of the herring gull (Pl. 16), or, notably, the red crown of the crane. Sometimes we find imaginative embellishments such as long tails, which are especially common in the later French manuscripts, or an artist would transfer a feature of one bird, such as the bustle-like secondaries of the crane, to another, so that one can only conclude, 'This is probably intended to be a stork, but the artist has drawn a bad crane.' On the rare occasions when professional ornithologists have been called upon to identify the birds in a single manuscript even they have often made mistakes, and it is sad to have to observe that art-historical studies contain many incorrect identifications.

Non-passerine birds
Cranes and other long-legged birds

The crane, now confined as a breeding bird in Europe to the countries round the Baltic, and seen only in small numbers on migration elsewhere, is almost certainly the commonest of all birds in English manuscripts, apart from the symbolic dove and eagle; I have seen it in more than 60. Either the red crown or the fluffy bustle is usually enough to identify the drawing, and the two together make identification certain. In cases where only the bustle is shown the artist has probably either been copying unintelligently or has added it to another bird. This confusion is especially common in bestiaries.

There are a number of cranes in manuscripts of around AD 1000, as early as any recognisable wild bird. B.L. MSS.Cotton Julius A. VI and Cotton Tib.B. V, both of which include a work known as 'The Marvels of the East', have a calendar at the beginning, illustrated with a scene for each month. In both, the theme for October is hawking (Fig. 3). The two scenes are very similar in layout, with one man on foot carrying his hawk, and another on horseback; between them is a group of birds, including a crane. Obviously, one of these pictures is copied

Fig. 3. *Crane (on ground between men); the scene is hawking, from the calendar for October. Hymnal, B.L. MS. Cotton Julius A.VI, f. 7v. English, early 11th century.*

from the other, or both come from a common prototype, but the crane in each of them is so well drawn in comparison with the hawks and other birds (probably ducks) that it must originally have been done from life.

From the time of the Bible of William of Devon in the mid-13th century onwards, cranes often appear as marginal decoration as well as occasionally in scenes of the Creation, of St. Francis preaching to the birds, and the Apocalypse (Pls.14,15). They vary from being well drawn to being mere sketches, recognisable only by their bustle, and they are often somewhat caricatured, the long legs and neck apparently encouraging a certain amount of artistic licence.

Cranes appear in continental manuscripts over the same period of time and about as frequently as in English works, but with an even greater tendency to poor drawing and caricature. With the exception of one mid-13th century Bible (Bodleian Lib. MS.Auct.D.1.17), probably French, I have not seen any really well-drawn examples earlier than the 15th century, when for instance we find one probably drawn from life in the Hours of Yolande de Lalaing from the Netherlands (Bodleian Lib. MS.Douce 93).

Most of the birds called storks by art-historians are in fact cranes. Storks are long-legged birds of a similar shape, but without the characteristic marks of the crane; moreover, the white stork, the common species of Europe, has a striking colour pattern: there is a broad black edging to the wing on an otherwise white body, and a red bill and legs, which make it easy to recognise. In addition to pictures, there is plenty of documentary evidence of the former presence of cranes in England (though it must be noted that in some counties the name crane was commonly given to the heron — a confusion which should not arise where the Latin name is used). On the other hand, there is no evidence for British breeding storks except for one 15th century record in Edinburgh. The stork, unlike the crane, does not appear in bills of fare, and was not commonly, if indeed ever, used in falconry. Yet the word 'storc' appears as a translation of the Latin *ciconia*

Fig. 4. *Stork on housetop. Matthew Paris, Chronica majora etc., B.L. MS. Roy. 14 C.vii, f. 4r. English, mid-13th century.*

Fig. 5. *Bill-clattering white stork. Bible, Fitzwilliam Museum MS. McLean 15, f. 183r. English, late 13th century.*

in the 8th century (Sweet 1885) and occurs occasionally thereafter. All this suggests that the stork, although not so common as the crane, was better known in the Middle Ages than now; and indeed the manuscripts confirm this.

The earliest drawing is a thumbnail sketch of a stork on top of a house in the British Library's mid-13th-century manuscript of Matthew Paris illustrating a journey to Italy (Fig. 4) It is uncoloured, but there can be no doubt of the identification; neither cranes nor herons frequent houses, and the drawing must have been done by someone who had seen the bird, though it could possibly have been remembered from foreign travel. The present distribution of the stork is disjunct, with populations in Spain and from the Rhine Valley eastwards. Its numbers have recently been falling, especially in the western part of its range, and it could well have been common in France and Italy in the Middle Ages. Next, there is a rather inaccurately coloured white stork in the McLean Bible of the late 13th century (Fig. 5). There is no white on its back, but the attitude is that of 'bill-clattering', a form of display in which the bird throws its head back until the beak is vertical or pointing downwards, and snaps its mandibles rapidly together. This display is unlikely to be forgotten by anyone who has seen it, or to be invented by anyone who has not. Most of the other pictures of storks show confusion with the crane. In the Bird Psalter, for example (Fitzwilliam Museum MS.2–1954,f.64v), we find a fairly competent drawing of a stork, but with curly secondaries. Finally, the Sherborne Missal has two good examples (pp. 19,366), the second actually labelled 'A stork'. In the Apocalypse with figures (Pl. 15) there is a bird that looks like a black stork, but since this is a much rarer species than the white, such an intention seems unlikely.

I have seen only a few poor storks in 13th century continental manuscripts, but there are more later, including one in a Flemish *Bartholomew* (Pl. 19) and eight, of varying quality, in an early 14th century Book of Hours (Trinity College Cambridge MS.B.11.22); two of these are well-drawn, one of them being in the bill-clattering position.

The commonest of all long-legged birds in nature is the heron. It has a drooping crest, but no striking colour-pattern, and is often impossible to identify in manuscripts except as an indeterminate bird that is neither a crane nor a stork. The earliest possible example is a bird in a Psalter of about 1170 at Glasgow (Hunter MS.229, f.42v); but although it has the correct blueish colour for a heron, it has the red beak and legs of a stork. The appearance of the other birds in this manuscript suggests, however, that the colours are meaningless, as is often the case at this date. There is a fair 'heyrun' in the Sherborne Missal (Fig. 6).

In continental manuscripts there are no good herons. The bird labelled 'a heryn' in the Pepysian Sketchbook (Magdalene College, Pepys MS. 1916, f.13v) is a crane.

The last, and perhaps the most interesting, of these long-legged birds is the spoonbill. It is completely white, except for a splash of yellow at the base of the neck, and has an unusually-shaped bill from which it gets its name. Its only regular breeding place in western Europe is now the Netherlands, but we know that it formerly nested elsewhere, including Norfolk. There is a good representation of it in the Peterborough Psalter (Pl. 30), a good head in the Creation scene of the contemporary Bromholm Psalter (Bodleian Lib. MS.Ashmole 1523, f.116v), and also half a dozen caricatures in which effective use is made of the bird's beak.

There is a good spoonbill in the Breviary of John the Fearless (B.L. MS.Add. 35311, f.333v) which was illuminated in Paris, probably by a Dutchman, in about 1415, but otherwise I know only of a few caricatures and one head in continental manuscripts, and one smudged bird that is probably a spoonbill amongst St. Francis' audience of birds on f.31v of the Montacute Psalter (C.U.L. MS.Add.4082), which is probably Flemish, of the late 13th century. A fuller investigation of Flemish manuscripts than I have been able to make might be expected to produce more. The bird still commonly referred to as a spoonbill on f.11v of the Pepysian Sketchbook is, if anything, a shoveler duck.

Grus, ciconia and *ardea* are in the *Aviarium* and some bestiaries derived from it, and for once the translations of these — crane, stork and heron — are certain. Cranes usually appear in the plural, *grues,* and accordingly the picture usually shows more than one bird, and illustrates the story in the text that, when cranes are resting, one stands on one leg holding a stone in the other, so that if it falls asleep the stone drops on to the foot on the ground and wakes the owner. In other contexts, we may usually assume that a bird

Fig. 6. *Heron. Alnwick Castle, The Sherborne Missal, p. 386. English, c. 1400.*

Fig. 7. Ciconia *(stork)*. Bestiary, Sidney Sussex College MS. Delta 5.15 *(James 100), f. 18r*. English, 13th century. Compare Fig. 5.

standing on one foot and holding a stone (usually spherical) is intended to be a crane. *Grus* is absent from French bestiaries except for B.L. MS.Harley 273 (Pierre de Beauvais), which perhaps accounts for the crane's comparative rarity in continental decoration.

Ciconia is present in all the bestiaries that contain *grus*, except that it is absent from the one at Alnwick, and from the bestiary pictures in Queen Mary's Psalter (B.L. MS.Roy.2.B.vii) (both of which are 'transitional'), and B.L. MS.Harley 273. It is occasionally recognisable as a white stork in, for example, Sidney Sussex College MS.100 (Fig. 7) and Bodleian Lib. MS. Ashmole 1511, f.6r. It often holds a snake or frog or fish in its beak, and frequently, too, has a crane's bustle. Sometimes, as in Fitzwilliam MS.379, f.21r, it is represented in a crouching attitude which suggests that it was drawn from a heron.

Ardea is rare in bestiaries, being illustrated only in those that follow the *Aviarium*, the 'second family' pairs B.L. MS.Harley 4751/Bodleian Lib. MS.Bodley 764 and Bodleian Lib. MSS.Ashmole 1511/ Douce 151, and in the third 'family'. It may be shown with a correct stance and holding a fish, but may have a crane's bustle.

Nothing that can be equated to a spoonbill occurs in the bestiaries, but those of the third 'family' have a bird called *butio* or *bucio,* which in Bodleian Lib. MS.Douce 88(ii) is also called *honocratulus*. The former word I have been unable to trace in any vocabulary, but *onocratulus* from the 11th century onward is translated raredumle, or bittern. None of the five drawings of *butio* is recognisable, some being black, some white, some having short legs, others long; that of the Douce MS. has a bustle.

Domestic birds

The common barnyard fowl was domesticated long before the Christian era, and there can be no doubt that it was kept throughout the period in question. Considering its decorative appearance the cock does not occur as often in manuscripts as one might expect – it is not as common as the peacock for example – but it appears in some of the earliest. A Canterbury psalter (B.L. MS.Cotton Vespasian A.I), usually dated to the second quarter of the 8th century, has several birds in initials, of which one (f.110r) is a fairly well-drawn, but rather unnatural, cock; it contrasts with all the others, which are sometimes, without much justification, called eagles, but which are in truth unrecognisable. Some look like birds plucked for the table. The Book of Kells (Trinity Coll. Dublin MS.A.I.6), which is probably a little later, has on more than one page a bird which to judge from its comb must be a cock (e.g. f.67r), facing others which are presumably intended to be hens. Since all are coloured in fantastic blues and greens they would not otherwise be identifiable.

Although the scenes of the Creation and the naming of the animals by Adam in illustrated Bibles mostly contain domestic mammals, the cock appears in only a fairly small proportion; one example is the Bible of Robert de Bello (Pl. 9, Fig. 12). It is much commoner in the same scenes in the Bible pictures prefixed to some bestiaries and in the illustrations of the Pentateuch, where I have found it in six out of 12, including Aelfric's Paraphrase (Pl. 8). It occurs very rarely in pictures of the ark. A cock appears in an illustration of Peter's denial (Luke 22) in an early Gothic Psalter dated before 1220 (B.L. MS.Roy.1D.x, f.5v).

Several Apocalypses contain illustrations of cocks. There is usually one sitting on the prow of the ship taking St. John to Patmos, and the bird occurs in other contexts in Trinity College Cambridge MS.R.16.2, Bodleian Lib. MS.Douce 180 and Yates Thompson MS.55 (now Los Angeles, Gulbenkian Collection). It may or may not be significant that all these Apocalypses contain owls (but not all those with owls have cocks).

A cock appears as decoration in 17 out of 62 psalters that I have examined, but in only three out of 35 of the Books of Hours and other prayer-books. It is most commonly found on the Beatus page (Psalm 1) but the reason may simply be that this page is usually the most lavishly decorated. It occurs in several other psalms, and as a line-filler in the Wilton Psalter (London, Royal College of Physicians).

In six of the English psalters I have examined, and in the Smithfield Decretals (B.L. MS.Roy.10E.iv), a cock is shown in a scene from Reynard the Fox, either being carried off by Reynard or as one of his audience while he preaches.

The occurrence of fowls in continental manuscripts is broadly similar to that in English ones. We begin to find examples at about the same time (Pl. 6, Ada Gospels); the cock is one of the birds that sit on the arches of canon tables (e.g. the French B.L. MS.Harley 2795, f.9v; cf. Pl. 7) and is still to be seen in the latest Books of Hours, for example the Flemish Hours of Engelbert of Nassau (Bodleian Lib. MSS.Douce 219–220) of c.1490. Reynard scenes occur, for example in the Metz Pontifical (Fitzwilliam Mus. MS.298) of c.1310.

Gallus the cock and *gallina* the hen come into the bestiaries from the *Aviarum,* and from then on are present in the majority. They are usually more or less recognisable, and sometimes have chicks.

Peafowl were kept in classical Rome, and representations of them occur in a few 4th-century Romano-Celtic mosaic pavements in Britain; whether they were present throughout Celtic and Saxon times we may never know. A bone was found in an undated but late Saxon site at Thetford, so it is possible that some did survive throughout the Dark Ages. The Latin *pavo* appears in an 8th century vocabulary with the translation 'pauua' (Sweet, 1885). There are representations of peafowl in art from about AD 700. Although these may have been copied from ancient manuscripts that had been imported, it is at least as likely that they are based on actual birds.

For the purposes of decoration the male bird is obviously far preferable to the female, and so it is usually the peacock that appears. He has two notable characters: a crest of about 24 pin-like feathers and a long train that bears eye-like markings and can be lifted and fanned out to make a dazzling display before the hen. Rather surprisingly, manuscripts more often show the tail trailing than erect. Somewhat doubtful peacocks in the Lindisfarne and Kells Gospels are shown in Pls. 3–5 and Fig. 8; more natural examples begin a little later. A Gospel book of around AD 1000, probably made at Winchester, has unmistakeable and fairly well-drawn peacocks on a canon table (Fig. 9). They are frequently seen in this position in Byzantine manuscripts, so these particular examples may in fact be copies, although they look rather more as if they were done from nature. A little later, about the middle of the 11th century, the Caedmon paraphrase of Genesis (Bodleian Lib. MS.Junius 11) has some sketchily-drawn birds which to judge from their shape and crests must be peacocks, both in Paradise (p. 11) and in the ark (p. 66)

Fig. 8. *Birds with double tails, probably based on peacocks. Lindisfarne Gospels, B.L. MS. Cotton Nero D.IV, f. 139r. English, c. 700.*

Fig. 9. *Peacock. Detail of canon-table of Gospel Book, Trinity College Cambridge MS. B.10.4 (James 215), f. 9r. English, c. 1000.*

where they have the double tail (cf Fig. 10). In the great Lambeth Bible of c.1130–40 we find for the first time two reasonably good coloured peacocks, worked into the loops of the initial S to the Prologue to the prophet Sophonias (Zephaniah) (Lambeth MS.3, f.308r). The upper one, moderately well-drawn, is walking to the left; the lower, rather better-drawn, is in pride. I can find no reference to the Resurrection, the event that the peacock is said to symbolise, in the book, and the only birds mentioned in the Vulgate text (2:14) are *onocratulus* and *corvus;* since neither of these could possibly be taken to mean a peacock, I conclude that the birds are pure decoration. The book was probably made at Canterbury, and James (1932) thought that the peacock became a mark of that scriptorium. In later years, however, the pictures of peacocks are so common, and the bird is so eye-catching, that I do not think this view can be maintained. Another 12th century book, the psalter (Hunter MS.229) already mentioned, which is from the north of England, also has a fairly good peacock in an initial (f.174r) that appears to be pure decoration.

In the 13th, 14th and 15th centuries there are many decorative peacocks, of varying quality. A Psalter, B.L. MS.Arundel 157, of *circa* 1200, has a fairly good bird in its pride in the initial D of Psalm 98 (f.82v). This is not one of the regularly illustrated psalms, and the only possible symbolism, that the peacock represents Christ, seems far-fetched. Of the psalters that I have seen, about a third from

Fig. 10. *Peacock showing the train with the short true tail below. Pepysian Sketchbook, Magdalene College Cambridge MS. Pepys 1916, f. 13r. Italian?, c. 1400.*

the 13th century have peacocks but only a fifth of those from the 14th. The majority, like those in Bibles, are in the margin or at the base of the page; only in Fitzwilliam MS.12 does one appear at the beginning of a psalm (No. 159, 'Dominus mea', f.159v), where it may have a symbolic meaning. There is also one on the Beatus page of the St. Omer

Psalter (Pl. 28). In the Amesbury Psalter (All Souls Coll. MS.6) and the Wilton Psalter, which were probably made in the same scriptorium, peacocks are used as line-fillers. Finally, there are peacocks in the 15th Century group discussed later in connection with owls (Pl. 39, Fig. 59).

Peacocks are even commoner in continental manuscripts, featuring in the decoration of early canon-tables (e.g. Rylands MS.10, 9th century, from Liège) and continuing to the end of the period. Sixteen out of 32 of the decorated Books of Hours that I have seen have them, against only seven of 35 English Books of Hours.

Pavo was not in the Greek bestiary, but had appeared by the early 12th century, and from then on is found in most books of each 'family'. It is sometimes, but by no means always, well drawn, and often shown with the tail erect, although the colours used are sometimes wrong.

The goose was also domesticated long before the Middle Ages; however, its farmyard form differs little from the wild grey lag goose (except that white forms occur), and therefore it seems probable that most representations are of the domesticated bird. For example, the grey geese on ff.87v and 134v of the Bird Psalter and the bird in the Pepysian Sketchbook, all of which have been identified as grey lags, are in my opinion probably tame.

Most geese appear as rather sketchily-drawn creatures, hardly distinguishable from ducks, swimming in ponds. The earliest I have seen is in a St. Albans Bible of the late 12th century at Cambridge (Corpus Christi Coll. MS.48, f.7v). Geese identifiable only by shape, and distinguishable from ducks only by size, appear in a number of illustrations from the story of Reynard the Fox. Geese are to be found in very few continental manuscripts.

The bestiary *anser* occurs in copies taken from the *Aviarium* but is afterwards illustrated only in two 'second family' pairs B.L. MS.Harley 4751/Bodleian Lib. MS. Bodley 764 and Bodleian Lib. MSS. Ashmole 1511/Douce 151, and in one 'third family' book (Bodleian Lib. MS.Douce 88 (ii)). It is usually somewhat conventional but in the Ashmole Bestiary is white with a red beak.

Ducks were certainly kept in the later Middle Ages; they are listed as domestic birds by Alexander Neckam in about 1190. The latin *anas* appears with the Anglo-Saxon translation 'ened' in the 8th century (Sweet, 1885).

Birds swimming in a pond which, although very sketchily drawn, give a fair impression of ducks, appear early, for example in B.L. MS.Harley 603 (Fig. 11). The scenes in this manuscript are copied from the earlier continental Utrecht Psalter (Rijksuniversitet Bibliotheek, script. eccl.484), but many details are different, and the ducks on f.4v are more like the real thing in the British Library manuscript than are those in Utrecht. Later on, domestic ducks tend to be abandoned in favour of wild ones, although they persist in scenes from Reynard the Fox.

Domestic ducks are a little commoner than geese in continental manuscripts, and in some later Books of Hours, there are fantastic birds that appear to be based on ducks.

Anas the duck is present in most 'transitional', 'second family', 'third family' and 'fourth family' bestiaries, and is usually conventional in appearance. In Corpus Christi Coll. Cambridge MS.53, a bestiary of the second 'family', there are two ducks, both white with red beaks (f.203v), a colouring which suggests, but does not prove, a domesticated form of the Aylesbury type.

The history of the domestication of the mute swan from the 13th century has been recorded by Ticehurst (1957). In art, the species is firmly recognisable only by the colour of the beak and the knob at its base, and I know of no manuscripts that show these earlier than the Bird Psalter of the late 13th century. There are, however, some earlier drawings of long-necked, relatively short-legged birds that are possibly intended for swans, for example in B.L. MS.Harley 603 (Fig. 11) and (a much better one) Aelfric's paraphrase (f.3v) of about 60 years later; and there are two quite fair ones, with red beaks but without knobs, on f.5r of the Trinity Apocalypse, which may be as early as 1230. There is a rather poor one in the Creation scene of the Bible of Robert de Bello of about the same date (Pl. 9, Fig. 12), and swans appear also in some Creation pictures. They continue to be found in small numbers up to the 15th century.

Fig. 11. *Ducks? cranes, swan? Psalter (Ps. 8), B.L. MS. Harley 603, f. 4v. English, early 11th century.*

Fig. 12. *Creation of birds, beasts and fish. The only bird certainly identifiable is an owl, but the long-necked one may be a swan. Bible of Robert de Bello, B.L. MS. Burney 3, f. 3v (detail of Pl. 9). English, early 13th century.*

The occurrence of swans in continental manuscripts seems to follow much the same pattern, although here they are perhaps less common. There is a good drawing in the French Sketchbook of Villard de Honnecourt of about 1250 (B.N.fr, 19093, f.4r). There are few in the late Books of Hours although they do appear in some written for Jean, Duc de Berri, who is said to have introduced tame swans into France, and who certainly adopted the bird for his badge.

Olor, or sometimes *cygnus,* the swan, is in the *Aviarium* and 'transitional' bestiaries, in nearly all those of the second 'family' and all the third and fourth, but not in the French ones except for Pierre de Beauvais (e.g. B.L. MS.Harley 273). The quality of the drawing varies, but is as good in a fairly early manuscript such as Sidney Sussex College 100, an Aviarium of the 13th century, as in many later ones. The swan is one of the few birds whose representation in bestiaries is perhaps as good as elsewhere.

Eagles and vultures

The eagle, and the dove representing the Holy Ghost, are the only birds that appear in manuscripts solely, or almost solely, as symbols or emblems. From an early date in the history of Christianity, not later than the 4th century, the four 'beasts' of Revelation 4:6–8 have been used to represent the four evangelists: the man St. Matthew, the lion St. Mark, the calf (or ox) St. Luke, and the eagle St. John. Eagles appear commonly at the beginning of St. John's Gospel, at the head of canon-tables, and throughout the Apocalypse, not only to illustrate the text but as symbols of the author, who was assumed in the Middle Ages to be the Evangelist. These symbols are usually connected with another vision, in Ezekiel 1:5–14 and 10:12–14, but a comparison of the two books shows that anatomically the two sets of creatures are very different, since in Revelation the four beasts are distinct while in Ezekiel the faces of man, lion, ox and eagle are attached to one body. The Ezekiel symbol appears for St. Mark (but not St. John) on a detached leaf at Avesnes (illustrated in Dodwell, 1959), and there are some traces of the influence of Ezekiel in the Book of Kells, but otherwise it is the Apocalypse that is followed, although seldom very closely. Each symbol ought strictly to have six wings and to be 'full of eyes within'. Out of 36 manuscripts with Johnian eagles only one Apocalypse (B.L. MS.Roy.15D.ii, 14th century) shows six wings, and another (Lambeth MS.75, 13th century) shows five. All the rest are more or less normal birds. The 'eyes' are equally uncommon, appearing only in the Book of Kells, where some of the eagles have rather peacock-like spots on their wings and tails (Pl. 5, Figs. 13, 14). It is clear that the artist did not in general follow the text.

It is unlikely that many artists were familiar with real eagles, and this must be especially true of England, where they are likely to have nested, if at all, only in the north. Since therefore the drawings must have been copies, it is surprising that some of them are as good as they are. Identification of the species of eagle intended is never possible, and sometimes the creature portrayed is quite fantastic, but generally the shape and appearance are fairly well conveyed. The eagle of Lindisfarne (Pl. 3) is one of the best, and suggests that the artist might possibly

EAGLES AND VULTURES

Fig. 13. *Eagle of St. John (holding a book). Detail of canon-table of The Book of Kells, Trinity College Dublin MS. A.I.6, f. 5r. English or Irish, late 8th century.*

have known the bird.

Vultures do not occur in English manuscripts, but there are some good Italian examples (Pl. 40).

Aquila and *vultur* in the bestiaries are discussed under Pl. 18.

It is said that *aquila* can also represent Christ or the Resurrection. I know of no illustrations where this can be stated with certainty to be the case, and only one or two where it is a possibility (Fig. 36).

Fig. 14. *Eagle of St. John, much influenced by peacock. The Book of Kells, f. 290v, detail of 'four symbols' page.*

Game-birds and wildfowl

Apart from the domesticated fowl and peacock, recognisable game-birds are rare in manuscripts. The only native species that is to be found over most of lowland Britain is the partridge; this bird, however, has no highly distinctive colours and so is unlikely to be identifiable except by its shape, which it shares with the much rarer quail. Queen Mary's Psalter has a picture of three birds being caught in a net (Fig. 15); they are small, but would do for partridges. Towards the end of the Trinity Apocalypse is the story, from the Golden Legend, of St. John and the partridge; the bird that must be intended to represent this (f.30v) would hardly be recognisable out of its context, since it is sitting on top of a tree, but it is more or less the right colour. There are two possible examples in the Bird Psalter (ff.38v, 77r).

The only continental manuscript in which I have seen partridges used as decoration is the North Italian Cocharelli Treatise, where there are both grey and red-legged birds (Pl. 40). Both species are also present in the Pepysian Sketchbook (Fig. 16). The drawings of *perdix* in the *De arte venandi cum avibus* of the Emperor Frederick II (Vatican, Pal.Lat.1071) are not recognisable as such in the facsimile of 1969 (I have not seen the actual manuscript), but a 15th century French treatise on falconry at Glasgow (Hunter MS.269, f.17r) has a fairly good partridge being attacked by a nondescript hawk.

The only good quail is in the Sherborne Missal, where its presence, in association with many northern species, suggests that it may

Fig. 15. *Partridges being caught in a net. Queen Mary's Psalter, B.L. MS. Roy. 2B.vii, f. 112r. English, early 14th century. Similar methods of catching birds are illustrated in Ray (1678).*

have been more widespread then than now, when it is found regularly only in some southern counties. There is a bird that is probably a quail, though it might be a partridge, in the Pilkington Charter (Fitzwilliam Museum), and another in the Flemish Romance of Alexander (Bodleian Lib. MS.Bodley 264, f.112r). A Spanish manuscript of the 11th century (Vatican Lib. Lat.5729, f.1r) and the French Rohan Book of Hours of the 15th (B.N.Lat. 9471, f.225v) illustrate the quails on which the Israelites fed in the wilderness (Numbers 11:31–32), but the birds are not like the real thing.

Perdix is in the Greek bestiary, and in

almost all the later ones, including the French. It is nearly always impossible, shaped like a crow or sparrow, and in B.L. MS. Egerton 613 (William the Norman) even like a wagtail. *Coturnix* is in one Aviarum bestiary, two 'transitionals', nearly all of the second 'family' except those without *perdix*, and all bestiaries of the third and fourth 'families'; it is no better drawn than *perdix*. It is missing from the French versions.

The date of the introduction of the pheasant into Great Britain is unknown. The earliest certain drawings of it are in the Sherborne Missal, where there are six, including both sexes, but there are possible examples in the Smithfield Decretals (f.42r) and the Luttrell Psalter (f.84v), both of which are about 60 years earlier. There is also a poor one, with incorrect head and tail, in the Windmill Psalter (New York, Morgan MS.102, f.2r; there is a coloured reproduction in Alexander, 1978). Nothing seems to be known about the origin of this manuscript, but it is said to be English and of the end of the 13th century. If this is the date and place of the pheasant on f.2, it is the earliest certain record of the bird in England, but it looks thoroughly French (especially in the tail) and of a later style than most birds of the 13th century. It might well have been added later.

There is a fairly good pheasant in the Belleville Breviary of Jean Pucelle of c.1325

Fig. 16. *Red-legged partridges. Pepysian Sketchbook, Magdalene College Cambridge MS. Pepys 1916, f. 10v; detail. Italian?, c. 1400.*

Fig. 17. *Probable capercaillie. Alphonso Psalter, B.L. MS. Add. 24686, f. 18r (detail of Pl. 23). English, before 1284.*

(B.N. Lat.10483-84, f.24v), and there are several in French Books of Hours (Pl. 44) and in a few other continental manuscripts of about the same period.

Fasianus appears in vocabularies of the 8th and 10th centuries (Sweet, 1885, and Wright, 1884) with the Anglo-Saxon translation 'wórhana'. This word is cognate with the German *Auerhuhn* and Dutch *auerhoen,* which are names for the capercaillie, which has the local Scotch name 'auer-caillie'. Since there is no evidence for the presence of the pheasant in Saxon times, this raises the ornithologically interesting possibilities that the capercaillie was present in southern Britain in the Middle Ages, and that the Roman *fasianus* was taken to be the same bird. There is a picture in the Alphonso Psalter that is more like a capercaillie than anything else (Pl. 23, Fig. 17).

I have seen no manuscript in which any of the other three British game birds — black grouse, red grouse and ptarmigan — can be identified with confidence. The 'mour hen' on p. 365 of the Sherborne Missal might just possibly be intended for a red grouse. The bird on f.77r of the Bird Psalter, called 'grouse or ptarmigan' in the Fitzwilliam Museum's list, is probably intended for a partridge, which is much more likely in a book illuminated in the west midlands.

In a number of Eastern manuscripts, e.g. the 6th century Rabula Gospels from Mesopotamia (Florence, Laurentian Lib. Cod.Plut.1.56) guinea fowl appear as decoration of the canon-tables. In a fairly extensive search through published reproductions of later canon-tables and a close examination of those directly available to me, I have found these birds in one manuscript only, Venice, Library of the Mechitharist Fathers 196, of the 12th century.

Page 370 of the Sherborne Missal contains a duck with dark grey back, red and white wing-bar, white ear-marks, and a light breast, labelled 'A bergandir'. This is a common name for the shelduck, and the colours are approximately correct for an immature bird. Much better, however, are a teal drake on p. 371 and a duck on p. 372, labelled respectively 'A Tel cok' and 'A Tel hen'. There is also a good teal drake on f.74v of the Bird Psalter (Pl. 48) and on f.51v another rather puzzling duck which the Fitzwilliam Museum's list and Dr. Hutchinson (1974) claim to be a drake smew. In my view the colours are not close enough to substantiate this identification.

The ordinary wild duck or mallard is so similar in colouring to many of its farmyard descendants that it is virtually impossible to say whether any of the good existing drawings, usually of the highly-coloured drake, was ever made from the wild bird; however, the ducks attacked by hawks must, when correctly coloured, as they often are (Pl. 22), be mallards.

The blue bird on f.11v of the Pepysian Sketchbook is probably a badly drawn shoveller.

The difficulty of distinguishing a grey lag goose from a domesticated bird has been

Fig. 18. *Barnacle goose. The Sherborne Missal, p. 390. English, c. 1400.*

mentioned above. The Sherborne Missal has what may be a grey lag (p. 391), labelled 'wyld goose', and a good barnacle goose labelled 'bornet' (Fig. 18); both are possible winter visitors to the Northumberland coast, but are less likely to have been found in Dorset, where the manuscript is said to have been made. 'Bornet' does not seem to have been recorded elsewhere, but would appear to be the same word as 'brant', which is sometimes applied to the barnacle goose.

Hawks and falcons

Hawking was a common sport for those who could afford it, from at least the 8th century onward, throughout the Middle Ages; but except for the *De arte venandi cum avibus,* we have no direct evidence of the species that were used. This book tells us much about falcons in Sicily, but little of that is necessarily applicable to northern Europe. The well-known list beginning 'An eagle for an emperor' derives in its usual form from the Boke of St. Albans of 1486, and cannot be traced back beyond the 15th century. Many of its species are unidentifiable, or if identifiable were unknown in England, and altogether the book has little if any relevance to fact (Yapp 1981). The medieval vocabularies show us that the distinction between the long-winged birds of prey or falcons (*falco*) and the short-winged birds of prey or hawks (*accipiter*) was well-known. This is to be expected, since the methods by which the two types naturally hunt their prey, and so those that are used in sport, differ. The term 'hawk' was probably used also, then as now, in an inclusive sense for all the diurnal raptors, including buzzards and kites, but not eagles.

The illustrations in manuscripts show that the short-winged hawks were much commoner in England than the falcons. The difference in the length of wing is one that artists, whether drawing from nature or copying, are on the whole likely to get right. The majority of the hawks shown in manuscripts are conventional representations, with the bird carried on the fist of a man or woman, sometimes on horseback. Amongst these I have found two that have distinctly long wings, and one in which, although the wings reach to the end of the tail as in a falcon, the tail itself is short. Some fifty others have short wings. Goshawks and sparrowhawks can hardly be distinguished in such pictures except by size, which is not a reliable character in medieval art, but if colours are shown they are different from those of the peregrine, the most likely falcon; in particular, hawks have a yellow iris, which many manuscript drawings of them show. There are five good English goshawks and one peregrine (Pls. 22, 48).

The only good peregrine that I have seen in a continental manuscript (except in Frederick II) is on f.41r of the Hours of

Giangaleazzo Visconti (Florence, Bibl.Naz. LF 22), where it can be recognised by its moustacial stripe; this manuscript is Italian, of about 1400. As in English manuscripts, indeterminate hawks are common.

There are also a few hawks with forked tails, which may represent kites (Pls. 10, 40).

Hawking as one of the 'Labours of the Months' is found from the 12th century to the 15th century. The month is usually May, but the picture is sometimes found as an illustration for April (e.g. C.U.L. MS.Dd.4.17), June (e.g. the Longleat Psalter) or October (Fig. 3). No doubt the scene was largely conventional, but there is so much variation in such details as the clothes and sex or status of the rider, and the size of the bird, that it must have been the general idea of hawking rather than a specific picture that was copied. It seems to have been especially English, since up to the end of the 12th century Webster (1938) could find no Italian examples, only two in 32 French calendars, but six out of nine English manuscripts. (He calls all the birds falcons, but this is not a reliable identification.)

Accipiter comes into the bestiary from the *Aviarium*. It is generally illustrated either by a picture that is barely recognisable as a hawk by its hooked beak, or by one without even that character. It is sometimes, as in the early B.L. MS.Roy.12C.xix of c.1187, shown biting its prey, but the latter is not itself identifiable. In another 12th century bestiary, Bodleian Lib. MS.Bodley 602(i), the hawk is shown seated on a block, and wears jesses. Exceptionally, Bodley 764, of the mid 13th century, shows a recognisable goshawk or sparrowhawk with barred breast held by a lady, while two mallard of roughly correct colouring swim in a pool behind. *Accipiter* is not shown in the French versions, and there are scattered examples of other 'families' that do not include it.

Some bestiaries of the third and fourth 'families' illustrate other hawks under the names of *capus* and *alietus*, but the pictures are not sufficiently detailed for us to identify them; in the vocabularies *alietus* means a sparrowhawk, a hobby or a merlin, and *capus* a muskett (a male sparrowhawk) or a 'wealhafoc' (which seems to have been a falcon). *Milvus* occurs in a few examples of every 'family'; common as the kite was, only in C.U.L. MS.Gg.6.5 is it shown with a properly forked tail, suggesting that the artist knew what he was drawing.

Owls

Owls are one of the most easily recognisable groups of birds. The flat face, giving binocular vision, and eyes and mouth surrounded by a circular, oval or heart-shaped pattern of feathers, the facial disc, give an owl a somewhat human look, which may be emphasised by the hooked beak being drawn to resemble a nose.

I have seen owls in nearly 60 English manuscripts, in some of which they occur on more than one page. A small number of Bibles and Bible pictures include an owl among the birds of the Creation scene (Pl. 9, Fig. 12). Three bestiaries have, as one of their preliminary pictures, an illustration of Adam naming the animals, among which is an owl. In Oxford St. John's College MS.61, f.2r the bird is unhorned, in MS.178, f.2r in the same library it has horns, while in the Alnwick Bestiary it is unhorned and holds a mouse in its beak. All these scenes include other birds, but there is a different collection in each. The only species common to the three being the domestic cock. All three manuscripts are 13th century; the one at Alnwick is 'transitional' and the others are 'second family'. Although the placing of this picture at the beginning of a bestiary could have a single source, it is such an obviously relevant idea that it might have occurred separately to different editors, and indeed the different groupings of birds suggest that this was so. (The only other bestiary containing this scene that I have examined, B.L. MS.Harley 3244, 13th century 'second family', has neither owl nor cock. The scene is also present in the English 'transitional' bestiary at Leningrad (MS.Qu.V.1), which apparently has an owl.)

Owls occur in 13 out of 33 English Apocalypses that I have seen, sometimes in the 'Call of the Birds', but also in other chapters. The majority are unhorned. Since the whole book is highly symbolic, the owls in it may have the general meaning of the 'bird of darkness' given to them in the bestiaries, but there seems to be no special reference to the text in the chapters where they occur.

I have seen few other biblical owls: an owl-like bird on f.133r of the 10th century Gospel Book with peacocks shown in Fig. 9; a square-headed one in brown, red and green holding a mouse by the tail in Jerome's Commentary on Isaiah of c.1130 (Durham Cathedral MS.B.II.8, f.10v); a rather poor one sitting on the tail of the big initial at the beginning of St. Luke in an early 13th century Gospel Book (Trinity College Camb. MS.B.5.3, f.111v); and another poor one at the beginning of St. Jude's Epistle in a 13th century Bible (Caius College Cambridge MS.361/442).

Apart from these few examples, the earliest example of an owl as pure decoration is in the earliest surviving English Book of Hours, which was illustrated by William de Brailes in the mid-13th century. This creature, however, is a monster, with human arms and hands (Fig. 19). From then on owls occur occasionally in about one fifth of psalters and less often in Books of Hours right up to the end of our period. Horned and unhorned birds are present in about equal numbers. The vast majority are not specifically identifiable; an exception is a tawny owl in the Ormesby Psalter (Pl. 24). Owls are very little used in non-biblical and non-liturgical manuscripts. There is one in the Pilkington Charter (Fitzwilliam Museum) and there are three from the 14th century: Bodleian Lib. MS.e.Mus. 60, f.86v (c.1320–30), the Smithfield Decretals, f.46r (c.1340) and Bodleian Lib.MS.Douce 35, f.25r (3rd quarter of the 14th century). A 'mixed set of Chronicles' (Trinity College Camb. MS.R.4.12, f.66r) has an owl-like bird among those being preached to by St. Francis. In the 3rd quarter of that century there is a group of five manuscripts with seven somewhat similar birds which are reasonably good representations of little owls; the original would have

Fig. 19. *Owl with human limbs, playing fiddle. Book of Hours, B.L. MS. Add. 49999, f. 55v. English, mid-13th century.*

been that shown in Pl. 39.

A few of the owls already mentioned are portrayed in the form of drolleries. That in Caius MS.361/442 is held by a monkey; the slightly monstrous one in B.L.MS.Add.49999 is playing the fiddle; that in the Bible of William of Hales at the beginning of the Book of Esdras is being shot at by an archer in a peaked cowl; and the Abingdon Apocalypse has on f.35v a monkey holding an owl on its fist like a knight carrying a hawk (Fig. 20). All these are 13th century. On f.1r of another 13th century Apocalypse (Lambeth MS.75), which some people think may be French, a monkey carrying an owl is riding a goat, and

Fig. 20. *Owl held by monkey in imitation of hawking. Abingdon Apocalypse, B.L. MS. Add. 42555, f. 35v. English, mid-13th century.*

Fig. 21. *Birds mobbing an owl used as a decoy. De Lisle Psalter, B.L. MS. Arundel 83, f. 14r (detail of Pl. 27). English, c. 1310.*

the same scene appears in the Luttrell Psalter (f.38r) of before 1340. There is possibly an element of symbolism here, since all these animals are sometimes thought to be evil. The Luttrell scene is on the Beatus page, the text of which begins 'Blessed is the man that walketh not in the counsel of the ungodly, nor standeth in the way of sinners, nor sitteth in the seat of the scornful.' The three animals might approximately symbolise these three types of man, but I can see no relevance to the beginning of the Apocalypse, where they are placed in Lambeth MS.75. It seems more likely that the scene is primarily an illustration for some lost story, comparable to Reynard the Fox (which, incidentally, is illustrated in both these manuscripts). Owls attacked by small birds or magpies (e.g. Bodleian Lib. MS.Rawlinson poetry 223, f.5r) are not necessarily symbolic, since such scenes were well known (Pl. 27, Fig. 21).

A peculiarity of a few medieval owls is that they have mammalian, or even human, pinnae (external ears); examples are the Luttrell Psalter, f.177v (Fig. 22), C.U.L. MS.Dd.8.2, f.27v, and Trinity College Camb. MS.O.1.57, f.2v. 'Long-eared owl' and 'short-eared owl' did not become well-established as names for two British species until the last century, and I have not been able to trace

Fig. 23. *Long-eared owl. Book of Hours of Etienne Chevalier, B.L. MS. Add. 16997, f. 21r (detail of Pl. 44). French, early 15th century.*

Fig. 22. *Owls with human ears. Luttrell Psalter, B.L. MS. Add. 42130, f. 177v. English, c. 1340.*

'eared owl' back further than Ray in 1678. (The Greek *hotos* was used by Aristotle for a horned owl, but I doubt if the Latin form of this was recognised in the Middle Ages as meaning 'eared'.) The presence of the ears in these pictures suggests that the phrase was in use as early as the 14th century, and that the artists were drawing purely from the name, without knowing what the actual bird was like.

Continental owls follow much the same pattern as English, one of the earliest, in the Bible of Philip the Fair of c.1290 (C.U.L. MS.Add.4083, f.70r), appearing in the margin of the Book of Deuteronomy. Identifiable species are as rare as in England, the only good ones I have seen being the two long-eared owls in the London Hours of Etienne Chevalier (Pl. 44, Fig. 23). Vaurie (1971) says that the Psalter of Bonne of Luxembourg (New York Metropolitan Museum of Art, Cloisters Collection) of c.1350 has a little owl, and on p. 162 of the Duke of Berry's 'Très Belles Heures de Notre Dame' (B. N. nouv. acq.lat.3093) of about 30 years later there is a probable barn owl.

Medieval bestiaries illustrate two species, *noctua* and *bubo,* which can be traced back to Aristotle. There can be little doubt that he meant by these the birds now called the little owl and the eagle owl, but by the Middle Ages all distinction had been lost. Medieval artists seem to have known that some owls have horns while others do not, but they did not apply the two names consistently. Figs. 24–27 show a representative selection of

Figs. 24–27. Noctua *in English bestiaries of the second 'family'.*

24. *B.L. MS. Add. 11283, f. 20r. Early 12th century. Crow-like.*

25. *B.L. MS. Harley 4751, f. 46v. Late 12th century. Short pinnae.*

BIRDS IN MEDIEVAL MANUSCRIPTS

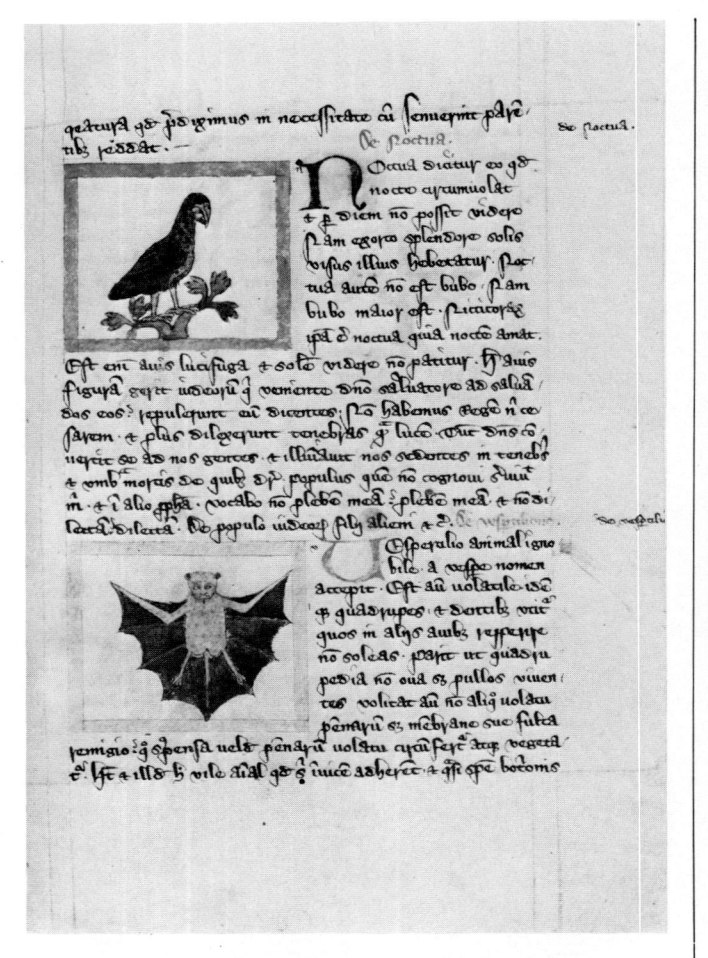

26. Bodleian Library MS. Douce 151, f. 57r. c. 1300. The noctua (upper picture) is parrot-like and has a rather human face. The bat (vespertilio) was regarded as a bird.

27. B.L. MS. Harley 3244, f. 54v. 14th century. Eared.

Figs. 28–31. Nycticorax *in English bestiaries.*

28. BL. MS. Roy. 12 C.xix, f. 49r. c. 1187. Transitional. Resembles cornix *(the crow) on f. 43r.*

29. Sidney Sussex College MS. Delta 5.15, f. 9r. 13th century. *'Aviarium'*. Eagle-like.

BIRDS IN MEDIEVAL MANUSCRIPTS

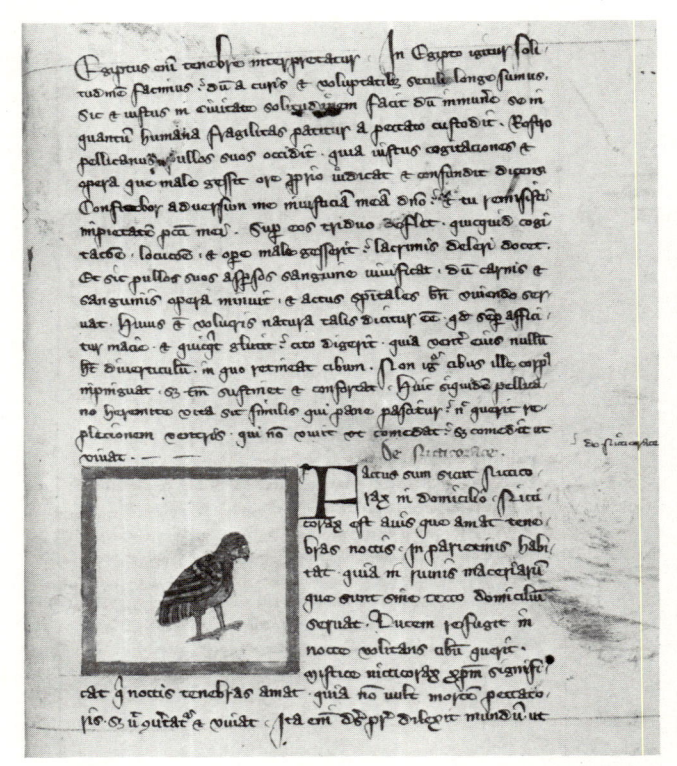

30. *Bodleian Library MS. Douce 151, f. 41r. c. 1300. Second 'family'. Striped and barred blue.*

31. *Trinity College Cambridge MS. 0.2.14 (ii) (James 1118), f. 38v. Rhymed bestiary of Guillaume le Clerc. 13th century. Stork-like, and translated as* fresei, *which Littré equates with* effraie, *the barn owl.*

noctua from 'second family' bestiaries; it is clear that although the list of subjects and the text are pretty much the same, there was much freedom of illustration. A few are not even recognisable as owls.

One should perhaps include under owls the bestiary *nycticorax*. This term, in its Greek form, is used by Aristotle, who says it is a name for the horned owl. It is one of the birds of the original Greek bestiary, where *noctua* and *bubo* do not occur, so there it probably represents an owl. By the Middle Ages all connection between it and owls had been lost, and the compilers and illustrators of the later bestiaries clearly had no idea of what they were writing about or drawing (Figs. 28–31). The name means literally 'night crow' or 'night raven', and is so translated in the vocabularies. (Its use as the Linnean name of the night heron, and White's use of this in his translation of the Bestiary (1954), are modern errors.)

Parrot

Only one species of parrot, the Indian rose-ringed parakeet, appears in manuscripts, and there is no evidence that any other was known. This bird is completely green apart from its red beak and feet, and, in the male only, its black and red collar. Ripley has suggested (in Hutchinson, 1974) that a similar African species may have been imported, but since this differs from the Indian species only in size and the absence of a collar from the cock, it cannot be distinguished in drawings. The earliest use of parrots as decoration is in the mid-13th century, in the books associated with William of Devon (Fig. 32), and they continue to be found both in England and on the continent, until manuscripts cease to be illuminated (Fig. 33). Many illustrations show the long tail split to the base, as it often is in aviaries.

Psitacus comes into the 'transitional' bestiaries, and is illustrated in all but a few of those of the second 'family' and in all those of the third and fourth. The parrot is absent from French bestiaries.

Fig. 32. *Parrots. Bible illuminated by William of Devon, B.L. MS. Roy. 1 D.i, f. 5r. English, 3rd quarter of 13th century.*

Fig. 33. *Parrot. Luttrell Psalter (Ps. 26, Dominus illuminatio), f. 51r. English, c. 1340. The beak, collar and feet are red.*

Pigeons

The vast majority of the representations of what are now called pigeons are of the symbolic dove which stands for the Holy Ghost, following the account of the Baptism of Christ in the Gospels (Matthew 3:16 etc.). It is found in any scene where the presence of the third person of the Trinity is appropriate, for example the Creation (where God the Father may be represented by a hand), the Annunciation, and of course the Baptism itself; in pictures of Pentecost (Acts 2) red lines usually run from the dove to the apostles. Sometimes the dove is hovering or standing at the ear of an evangelist or other saint as he writes (Fig. 34). In all these illustrations the bird is usually shown flying, and the representation of a flying bird is difficult. Nevertheless, the jizz is usually more or less accurate for a domestic pigeon, which suggests that although there was much copying and following of tradition, a faithful portrayal was maintained through the artists' familiarity with the

Fig. 34. *Dove representing the Holy Ghost descending to King David. Psalter (Ps. 1, Beatus), B.L. MS. Cotton Tiberius C.VI, f. 30v. English, mid-11th century. The dove is conventional except that it has no nimbus.*

Fig. 35. *Dove as Holy Ghost, held by the hand of God the Father. Psalter, B.L. MS. Cotton Tiberius C.VI, f. 15v. The dove is in blue, black and brown, and the scene represents Pentecost; red lines run to the apostles.*

bird. It is usually white with red feet, although other colours and attitudes are sometimes seen. For example, B.L. MS.Cotton Tib.C.VI, a Psalter of the mid-11th century, has a conventionally white dove on f.30v (Fig. 34), and on f.15v, for Pentecost, one that is blue, black and brown and held upside down by the tail; four fingers of what is presumably the hand of God the Father are visible (Fig. 35). Though the bird can hardly be flying, the positioning of the wings gives the impression that it is struggling to get free. Since this is one way in which birds are often held, the picture was perhaps drawn from life. These two doves are unusual in that they are not nimbed.

Occasionally, especially in early works, the dove appears to have been unfamiliar to the artist; at any rate, he has drawn a bird that is not a dove. In one 11th century Bible, for example, there is a bird in a Creation scene that looks more like an eagle than a dove, although the context suggests that it is the latter (Fig. 36). It seems more likely that there was an ignorant mistake in the drawing than that an eagle was used here as a symbol for the Holy Spirit, or, as has sometimes been suggested, for Christ. Similar and even clearer examples of the same error occur in Saxon and Norman sculpture.

By a slightly blasphemous extension of the symbolism, the dove comes to represent the soul of a righteous man, and is shown leaving his mouth or nostrils in death, or being carried up to heaven by angels (e.g. C.U.L. MS.Dd.8.2, f.21r).

Another scene commonly illustrated,

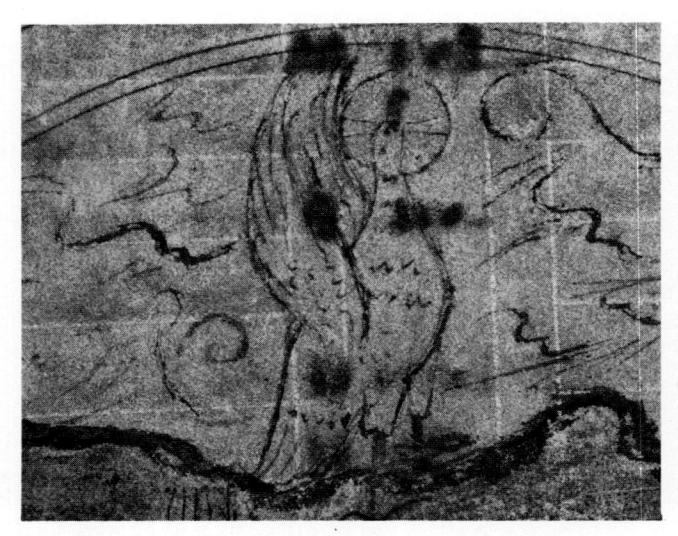

Fig. 36. *Eagle-like bird probably intended to represent a dove. Bible, B.L. MS. Roy. 1 E.vii, f. 1v. English, mid-11th century. Detail of Creation.*

where the bird has at most only a secondary symbolic significance, is Noah's release of a dove from the ark (Pl. 9). In a few sets of Bible pictures the Presentation in the Temple is shown. The accompanying sacrifice ought to be a 'A pair of turtle doves or two young pigeons' (Luke 2:24; in the Vulgate *turturum* and *pullos columbarum)*, but in none that I have seen are the birds any more than unidentifiable heads in a basket or bowl. In Eton MS.177, f.3v there are, in defiance of the text, three of them.

A few pigeons of other species are used in decoration, but they are rare. There is a good wood pigeon in the Alphonso Psalter (Pl. 1) and two possible stockdoves in the St. Omer Psalter (Pl. 28). The bird held by the Virgin in the Lambeth Apocalypse (MS.209, f.48r) might be intended to represent a turtle dove.

The symbolic dove occurs, as one would expect, in continental manuscripts just as it does in those made in England. The only good decorative member of the family that I have seen is a turtle dove in the London Hours of Etienne Chevalier (Pl. 44), and there are a few other French and Flemish manuscripts with long-tailed birds that look as if they belong to the same species. It is a bird that has spread north during the 19th and 20th centuries, but is still common in England only in the South-East. It is possible that it was scarce or entirely absent here in the Middle Ages.

Columba was one of the birds of the original Greek bestiary, and it occurs in all the later ones, except for the French versions and a few that are obviously defective. The one point in the text which the artist generally seizes on is that the birds are of various colours, and three or more, illustrating this, are usually shown. The birds are never really recognisable as doves. In B.L. MS.Harley 4751 there are three, sitting in a three-hole dove-cot.

Turtur also is one of the original birds, and is present in all but a few of the later bestiaries, including the three copies of William the Norman, which are without pictures of *columba* (B.L. MS.Egerton 613, Bodleian Lib. MS.Bodley 912 and Fitzwilliam Mus. MS.McLean 123). It is never recognisable and sometimes quite absurd in appearance. In some manuscripts, several birds, usually sitting in a tree, are shown.

Sea-birds

After the devastation of Lindisfarne in 793 no known centres for the production of manuscripts were on the English sea-coast, so it is not surprising that few sea-birds appear in them. On the contrary, it is perhaps surprising that there are at least two good gulls and two doubtful ones. A common gull in the Alphonso Psalter is shown in Pl. 1 and Fig. 37, and a herring gull from a 13th century Apocalypse in Pl. 16; the others, both herring gulls, are in Fitzwilliam Mus. MS.McLean 15, f.269v (a fairly certain identification) and on f.75v of the Bird Psalter (where the identification is more doubtful). All these were made at the end of the 13th century; the Alphonso Psalter is perhaps East Anglian, the Fitzwilliam Bible has been ascribed to York, and the Psalter to Winchcombe. Did gulls penetrate inland in the 13th century as they do now, but did not in the 19th century, or is there perhaps some hitherto unnoticed connection between these manuscripts?

The bird labelled 'A mew' on p. 392 of the Sherborne Missal, which ought, according to the modern meaning of the word, to be a gull, is not recognisable as such, unless perhaps it is intended to represent an immature herring gull.

Fig. 37. *Common gull. Alphonso Psalter, f. 11. (detail of Pl. 1). English, before 1284.*

The only English gannet is in the Sherborne Missal (Fig. 38), as is the only cormorant (Fig. 39), except that there is a

BIRDS IN MEDIEVAL MANUSCRIPTS

Fig. 38. *Gannet. The Sherborne Missal, p. 369. English, c. 1400.*

Fig. 39. *Cormorant. The Sherborne Missal, p. 368. English, c. 1400.*

cormorant-like bird with a spoonbill's beak in the 13th century History of St. Edward at Cambridge (C.U.L. MS.Ee.3.59, f.14r), which is connected with Matthew Paris.

All the 'pelicans' in English manuscripts are conventional (Pl. 11).

Sea-birds are even rarer in continental manuscripts than in English. There is a good herring gull in the Pepysian Sketchbook (f.11v). In addition to the conventional pelicans there are genuine ones in the *De arte venandi cum avibus* (f.42v) and in the Italian Cocharelli Treatise (Pl. 41).

Apart from *pelicanus*, the only sea-birds in bestiaries are *mergus* or *mergulus*, which is present in all those of the third 'family', and *bernace*, the barnacle goose, an account of which, taken from Giraldus Cambrensis, occurs only in B.L. MS.Harley 4751 and Bodleian Lib. MS.Bodley 764, which are discussed under Pls. 17 and 20. *Mergus* and *mergulus* are variously translated in the vocabularies: 'fugeldoppe' and 'scealfer' and variants of these in the 11th century, 'cormorant' and 'coot' in the 15th. The pictures in Westminster Abbey MS.22 and C.U.L. MS.Kk.4.25 are duck-like. It seems that the compilers knew that the birds were of diving habit, but no more, and we are unfortunately no better informed.

Waders

I place here a number of species, all but one belonging to a single natural order, which have in common the fact that, with the exception of the woodcock, they live in open country or near water, and, with the same exception, are not found in heavily wooded areas. Most have relatively long legs and beaks.

The woodcock can be distinguished from the snipe not only by its size but by the transverse barring on the head. This is well shown in a few 14th century pictures (Pls. 15, 33, Fig. 40), and there are also half a dozen others that are less good. Some of these may perhaps represent snipe, but there are no contemporary drawings of this bird of which I can be certain; the Sherborne Missal has a bird labelled 'A scnite' (Fig. 41) which is correctly differentiated from a woodcock on p. 374. No doubt woodcocks were more easily caught than snipe ('springes to catch woodcocks', *Hamlet* 1:5, and at least four other references in Shakespeare) and were more valuable for the table when caught.

There is a bird labelled 'woodcoke' in the Pepysian Sketchbook (f.10v) but its head is not barred. Otherwise, in continental

Fig. 40. *Woodcock. Apocalypse, Lincoln College MS. 16, f. 174v, the 'Call of the Birds'. Jay, bullfinch, crane, owl also shown.*

manuscripts I have seen only a good, but slightly caricatured, example in the probably Flemish Book of Hours Trinity College Cambridge MS.B.11.22, f.159v, and another which is probably a woodcock, in a French Psalter C.U.L. MS.Add.4085, f.37v. Both are c.1300.

An historical chronicle at Cambridge

Fig. 41. *Snipe. The Sherborne Missal, p. 373. English, c. 1400.*

Fig. 42. *Curlew? standing on foliage. Chronicle of England, Trinity College Cambridge MS. R.17.7 (James 993), f. 10r. English, early 14th century.*

contains a picture of a bird that looks like a curlew with long curved beak standing on foliage (Fig. 42) and there is another possible curlew in a 15th century French Book of Hours at Manchester (Rylands MS.164, f.27v).

There is what appears to be a lapwing on the ground below God the Father in the Creation scene in the Holkham Bible Picture Book (Pl. 10), and a rather better one in a 14th century manuscript of the poem 'Lancelot du lac' (Fig. 43). The latter is shown sitting on a spray, which is not the habit of lapwings, but this kind of artistic conceit need not worry us unduly; most of the half dozen birds in the manuscript are more or less caricatured, and two of them, like the lapwing, are perched on foliage. I have seen continental lapwings only in reproduction: in the Psalter of Bonne of Luxembourg. (f.321v, c.1350) and (a rather similar but better example) in the Golden Bull executed for the Emperor Wenceslas in about 1390 (Vienna, Österreichisches Nationalbibliothek Cod.338, f.1r). The other birds on this page (great tit, bullfinch, goldfinch) are typically French of the period, which is not surprising in view of the closeness of the French and Bohemian courts (Wenceslas was Bonne's nephew).

The Pepysian Sketchbook has a possible moorhen (f.12r) and also, perhaps surprisingly, an unmistakeable water rail (Pl. 2). There is a probable moorhen in a pond in the Romance of Alexander at Oxford.

None of the birds in this section strictly appears in a bestiary, but at some time the

Fig. 43. *Lapwing? sitting on spray. Lancelot du lac, B.L. MS. Roy. 20 D.iv, f. 207r. English, 14th century.*

bird called *upupa* became recognised first by artists and then by lexicographers as being the lapwing. The reason for this is that it is described as having a crest, and, as Englishmen did not know the real *upupa*, or hoopoe, they gave it one that they knew, either that of a peacock or that of a lapwing (Fitzwilliam Mus. MS.379, Corpus Christi College Cambridge MS.53, Bodleian Lib. MS.Douce 88(ii)), and the jizz makes it resemble that bird.

Miscellaneous non-passerines

The cuckoo, with its distinctive song and onomatopoeic name in many languages, was certainly well-known in the Middle Ages, but it has no very distinctive physical features, and there are no certain pictures of it. The list kept at the Fitzwilliam Museum claims one on f.63r of the Bird Psalter, but it has been identified by some ornithologists as a fieldfare or a dove. David Lack found three on f.11v of the Pepysian Sketchbook, but none of these birds looks to me like a cuckoo. There is another possible example in the Romance of Alexander in the Bodleian Library (f.165r).

Cuculus is illustrated in some third and fourth 'family' bestiaries, but is unrecognisable; in Fitzwilliam Mus. MS.254 (f.29v), for example, it is red and green, and in C.U.L. MS.Gg.6.5 (f.71r) it is blue, with a long beak.

The hoopoe occurs regularly as a vagrant in England, but only rarely breeds; the average for the past century appears to be a little more than once in ten years. Accordingly, there are no certain pictures in English manuscripts. In the Peterborough Psalter (Pl. 29) and in a Book of Hours of about 1300 at Cambridge (Christ's College MS. 8, f 59r) there are grotesques, each of which has a crest that suggests that it might be based on a genuine hoopoe. As there is also a bird rather like a hoopoe carved on a bench-end at Great Gransden (formerly Huntingdonshire, grid reference TL/271556), and another painted on a wall at Barton near Cambridge (TL/408557), it is possible that some English artists were familiar either with the bird or with some of the good French and Italian pictures of it from the 14th and 15th centuries (Pl 40, Fig. 44). In de Grassi's sketchbook (see notes on Pl. 2) there is an excellent bee-eater.

As I commented above, in discussing the lapwing, English bestiaries did not recognise *upupa* as the hoopoe, but a French copy of the rhymed bestiary of William the Norman (Fitzwilliam Museum MS.20, f.50v) contains three of the very best pictures of this bird.

The kingfisher is not, in view of its brilliant colours, so common in manuscripts as might be expected, and the colours are seldom well reproduced. Examples are shown in Pls. 1 and 15, and the only others I know are in the Luttrell Psalter (f.61r) and the Sherborne Missal (p. 383). There are rather more continental kingfishers, mostly 14th or 15th century, e.g. B.L. MS.Stowe 17, f.52r, Trinity College Cambridge MS.B.11,22, f.19r, Bodleian Lib. MS.Bodley 264, f.29r, Rylands MS.164, f.179v.

I am by no means sure that the *halcyon* of Aristotle really was, as is commonly said, the kingfisher, but however that may be the Latin *alcion* was certainly not recognised as such by the compilers and illustrators of the 'second family' and later bestiaries, for it usually has webbed feet and sometimes long legs and an exaggeratedly long beak. The *martinetas* of Giraldus are discussed under Pl. 20.

The green woodpecker is rather more common in decoration than the kingfisher, but is similarly not very correct in its colouring. An exception is found in the Alphonso Psalter (Pl. 1), and there are fairly good examples in the Bird Psalter (f.9r) and the Sherborne Missal (p.216), as well as a few others that are less good. Quite a good one, labelled 'picus' is in the scene of the 'Call of the Birds' in the Alexdrandrine Apocalypse at Cambridge (Pl. 14).

The green woodpecker is even less common in continental manuscripts, occurring in only four out of my series of 33 Books of Hours; in one of these, the London Hours of René of Anjou, however, there are no fewer than six (Pl. 47). To some extent its place is taken by the great spotted woodpecker, which I have seen in no English manuscripts (Pl.42). These last three or four birds, which are usually placed close together in schemes of

Fig. 44. *Hoopoes. Cocharelli, Tractatus de vitis septem, B.L. MS. Egerton 3127, f. 1v (detail of Pl. 40). Italian, late 14th century.*

MISCELLANEOUS NON-PASSERINES

classification, are sometimes associated in French manuscripts. A Book of Hours of c.1400 (B.L. MS.Add.29433), for example, has kingfisher, hoopoe, green woodpecker and what may be a great spotted woodpecker, and two of the species often occur together.

I have seen no lesser spotted woodpeckers.

Picus of the *Aviarium* and later bestiaries is assocated with *pica,* the magpie, with which it has no similarity apart from the name. The only illustration that I have seen is in the 'third family', Westminster Abbey MS.22, f.39r, where it is pink, with a very large beak. According to McCulloch (1962) there is also a picture in the French bestiary of Pierre, Paris Arsenal MS.3516.

In the Middle Ages the ostrich must have been fairly abundant around the southern and eastern shores of the Mediterranean, and so it is surprising that it seems to have been entirely unknown in western Europe. It is in most bestiaries under the name of *assida* or *struthio,* and is described as having feet that are cloven, or like those of a camel. The pictures generally show it with hooves like a sheep, but the body may be almost any shape whatsoever. Fig. 45 shows an extreme case, where the artist has given the bird a sheep's head to match its feet. This is a psalter, and is one of the half dozen examples of the bestiary ostrich used as decoration.

Fig. 45. *Bestiary* assida *(ostrich) with cloven hoof and sheep's head in initial C. Psalter, Trinity College Cambridge MS. B.11.4 (James 243), f. 144r. English, mid-13th century.*

Passerine birds
Crows

The typical members of the family Corvidae are black all over, and so unlikely to be distinguished in medieval drawings, since such points as size and the wedge-shaped tail of the raven would seldom have been recorded or observed. Only the red or yellow beak of the chough and perhaps the light eye of the jackdaw are characters of the kind that one might expect the medieval artist to have noticed. The bird translated in the English Bible as raven is often shown in illustrations of the ark, from Aelfric's 11th century paraphrase onwards (Pl. 9), and there may be similar birds in the Creation scenes (Pls. 8,9, Fig. 12). All-black birds in the 'Call of the Birds' may appropriately be taken to be either ravens or carrion crows (Pls. 14,16, Fig. 2). Large birds in country scenes following men working on ploughed fields are presumably intended to be rooks. In the Luttrell Psalter, where they are pecking at seed corn (f.170v) and following a harrow (f.171r), they are reasonably well-drawn, but in a 12th century manuscript of Bede's 'Life of St. Cuthbert' (Univ. Coll. Oxford MS.165, p. 61), two of the birds eating the corn are brownish-purple, one is red and one green; they are described only as *volucres* (birds). Two pages later *corvi* (ravens), bringing the saint a gift, are completely black. A number of French and Flemish manuscripts of the 14th century contain well-drawn hoody crows; examples are a Flemish Bartholomew (Pl. 19) and the 'Très Riches Heures' of John, Duke of Berry (Chantilly, Musée Condé MS.1284, f.2v). The hoody is at present only a winter visitor to Flanders and northern France. While the 'Très Riches Heures' show a winter scene with snow, the Flemish manuscript shows a street scene, which includes a white stork, which is a summer migrant; was the artist conflating seasons as well as birds – there are ten identifiable species and a few others – or did the breeding range of the hoody extend further west on the continent than it does now? There are hoodies in the Vatican manuscript of the *De arte Venandi,* which is to be expected, as they are the normal crows of Italy. I know none in English manuscripts.

The only certain jackdaw is that shown in Pl. 29. There is a chough in the Holkham Bible Picture Book (Pl. 10), and perhaps others in the Bird Psalter (f.154v), in the Peterborough Psalter at Brussels (Pl. 29), and the French Rohan Hours (B.N. Lat. 9471, f.7r).

The jay appears commonly as decoration from the 13th century onwards (Pls. 24,29), and also in Apocalypses (Pls. 13,15). It is sometimes well-drawn, but at others recognisable only by the blue wing-bar. There is evidence that it was a common cage-bird, taught to speak, so that it was clearly attractive and easy to draw. Magpies were also kept, and there are even more examples of these than of jays. Though less decorative, they have a simple black and white pattern. An odd feature of some of them is that the long tail is shown split to the base. It is always shown in modern books as 'graduated' – that is, with the central pair of feathers longest and the others receding step by step on each side. This is formally correct, but I have twice seen a magpie, when alighting on the top of a tree, divide its tail in exactly the way shown in medieval drawings (compare the parrot, above). Neither the jay, nor, except for its traditional occurrence in Apocalypses, the magpie, is common in continental manuscripts.

Medieval man had names for ravens, crows, jays and magpies, and a smaller corvid called 'ceo' and another called 'hroc', or variants of these. 'Ceo' became chough, but the name was almost certainly used either originally or concurrently for what is now called the jackdaw, so that medieval references can give us no information about the distribution of these two. 'Hroc' became rook, but since – to name but a few examples – neither Shakespeare nor Tennyson, nor C. S. Lewis nor Victoria Sackville-West could tell rooks from crows, or even apparently knew that there are two species, it seems unlikely that there was any clear distinction in the Middle Ages. The Latin names are equally confused. *Corvus* or *corax* (which is Greek) was in the original bestiary, and is generally and probably correctly translated as raven, while *cornix,* the crow, is in most 'transitional' bestiaries and those of the second and third 'families'. It is placed next to *corvus,* and the pictures of the two are usually indistinguishable. *Monedula* is in all five 'third family' bestiaries, but only in Fitzwilliam Mus. MS.254 does it have a light eye that suggests that it might have been drawn from a jackdaw; the jizz here is also good. *Graculus* is in the *Aviarium* and in a few 'second family' bestiaries and some of those of the third. What exactly it was we do not know; by the 15th century the word meant jay, at the time of the bestiaries it is not to be found in the vocabularies, while in the 11th and 8th centuries it is translated 'hroc' or 'hrooc'. It may equally have been a jackdaw, chough or jay. The pictures do not help, being completely unrecognisable. *Pica,* the magpie, is present in the majority of bestiaries from the 'transitional' group onwards; it is usually black and white, but otherwise rather poor, the drawings in the third 'family' being on the whole better.

Finches and similar birds

The goldfinch is by far the commonest of all small birds in illuminated manuscripts – it is present in 29 – reflecting, no doubt, the frequency with which it was kept in cages, as it still is in many parts of Europe. Most of the well-known pages with birds show it (Pls. 1,10,11,15,24,27,29,33, most of which are psalters). The representation in many of them is good, and all are recognisable. Goldfinches are even more common in continental manuscripts – I know of them in 40 – especially in French Books of Hours of the 15th and 14th centuries, but here they appear as isolated marginal decorations rather than as elements in one well-designed page, and some are clearly rapid copies; in Trinity College Cambridge MS.B.11.22, for example, there are at least 10, which range in quality from good to poor (Pl. 31). Another difference is that many French goldfinches are caricatured (as are other birds), for example with long beaks as in the 14th century St. Omer Hours (B.L. MS.Add.36684), or long tails as in the Hours of Marguerite de Foix (Victoria and Albert Museum MS.Salting 1222), of the late 15th century. This last manuscript is unusual in twice showing a goldfinch sparring in the air with a great tit. Such interspecific rivalry does take place – I have myself seen it between chaffinch and a coal tit – so that the drawings may be based on observation in the large aviaries common in France at that time.

There are several bullfinches, although not as many as there are goldfinches, and again many of them are featured in whole decorative pages, especially in psalters; indeed, they are often on the same pages as goldfinches (Pls. 1,10,11,27). Both sexes may be shown. Very unusually, a picture of Adam naming the animals prefixed to the 'second family' bestiary St. John's Coll. Oxford MS.178 has two very good cock bullfinches and two goldfinches among his audience.

In continental manuscripts also bullfinches are much less common than goldfinches. A few of the well-known Books of Hours have them, and there are other scattered occurrences, for example in the Pepysian Sketchbook (f.11r), a poor one in Trinity MS.B.11.2 (f.131r), a cock in Bodleian Lib. MS.Bodley 264 (f.9r) and a series of poor ones in a French Apocalypse of the early 14th century (B.L. MS.Add.17333).

All ornithologists would agree that the

chaffinch is present in much larger numbers and in a wider variety of habitats than either the goldfinch or the bullfinch. It is not so highly coloured, and although the colours and pattern are distinctive, so that it is easy to recognise in the field, many of the drawings are somewhat doubtful. The only one of the well-known ornithological psalters in which it occurs is the Fitzwilliam Bird Psalter (Pl. 33), where the picture usually called a chaffinch might represent a linnet or even a robin. I have recorded a total of only six occurrences, in five English manuscripts, including a picture of both cock and hen, labelled 'cayfinch', in the Sherborne Missal (Pl. 37). By contrast, I have recorded it in seven French, six Flemish and two Italian manuscripts, of which one is 16th, seven are 15th and seven are 14th century. It seems possible that this state of affairs, the opposite of that for the bullfinch, derives from a different distribution of the species in England then and now. The chaffinch has spread into the northwest of Scotland only during the past hundred years or so, and it still leaves the woods, its natural habitat, in winter. It may therefore have been rare in England in the Middle Ages.

Greenfinches are even rarer in manuscripts than chaffinches. There are two in the Ormesby Psalter (Pl. 26) and a few possible examples in one early 15th century French manuscript.

In the Gray-Fitzpayn Hours are a cock and a probable hen hawfinch (Pl. 32). There is a bird with a crossbill's beak, and with colouring (but not jizz) that would pass for an immature bird, in a late 15th century Flemish manuscript (Fig. 46).

Fig. 46. *Crossbill? Black Hours of Charles the Rash, Duke of Burgundy, Vienna, Österreichische Nationalbibliothek Cod. 1856, f. 32v. Flemish, 1466–76.*

Neither the birds called 'tarin' (probably the serin) in Trinity Hall Cambridge MS.12, f.126v, nor Matthew Paris's crossbills (Corpus Christi College Camb. MS.16, f.252v) are recognisable. The last look as much like larks as anything else, and the artist may have been misled by the text, which says that the birds with crossed bills that invaded the country and fed on apple pips were larger than larks (*alaudis parum majores*).

I have found four English birds that are probably linnets, although as they are little more than brown birds with reddish breasts it is not possible to be sure that they are not poor attempts at chaffinches or robins; that on p. 391 of the Sherborne Missal is labelled 'linet'. I have seen them in two French manuscripts, the London Hours of Etienne Chevalier (Pl. 44) and a Book of Hours in the Rylands Library (MS.164), which contains four, one of which is the best of all.

The only finch that I have seen in a bestiary is *carduelis*, in one of the third 'family' (Westminster MS.22), and in the fourth 'family'. In neither is the drawing recognisable – in the Westminster manuscript the bird is white.

Buntings are now placed in a separate family from the finches, but ecologically they are very similar. Hutchinson (1974) claims that a bird in the Ashridge *Historia Scholastica* (B.L. MS.Roy.3.D.vi, f.93r) is a bunting, presumably a yellowhammer, and as it has a yellow head and breast and is more or less the right shape, it could be; I prefer to suspend judgement, since yellow was often applied meaninglessly, as mere decoration. Two birds on ff.11r and 11v of the Pepysian Sketchbook look to me more like buntings, but I am not sure of their species. Lack called both of them ortolans, but they are not alike, and the former might equally well be a blackheaded bunting.

Sparrows (in the narrow sense) are even further from the finches, but also resemble them ecologically. The only certain ones are named: in the Alexandrine Apocalypse *passer* (Pl. 14) and in the Sherborne Missal 'sparwe cok' and 'sparwe hen'. There are a few other possible candidates, mostly rather unlikely, in English, French and Flemish manuscripts; and the Pepysian Sketchbook contains a fairly good cock.

Passer appears in scattered copies of the bestiary: in some of the *Aviarium*, in three of the second 'family', one of the third, and in the only 'fourth family' manuscript. Only in Fitzwilliam Museum MS.379 (second 'family') and in the fourth 'family' is the drawing recognisable as a house sparrow.

Swallows

The two species of swallow, three of martin, and three of swift found in continental Europe are hardly distinguished by the ordinary person, and the men of the Middle Ages were no better. The hirundines that blinded Tobit are discussed under Plate 12 (cf. Figs. 47–50), and apart from these and the bestiary birds there are none in English manuscripts except one possible candidate in the Holkham Bible Picture Book (Pl. 10). In the Rothschild Canticles (Yale University, Beineke Lib. MS.404, f.5r) probably made in the Netherlands at about the same time as the Holkham Picture Book, a swallow chases a fly. Around 1335–50, swallows appear as decoration in at least one Flemish and two French manuscripts: Bodleian Lib. MS.Bodley 264, ff.198r,198v, which was made at Bruges, the Hours of Jeanne de Navarre (B.N.n.acq.Lat.3145, f.55v) and the Missal of St. Denys (V. and A. MS.1346/1891, f.284v). There are four rather poor ones in the Duke of Berry's 'Grandes Heures'.

Hirundo is in the *Aviarium* and the bestiaries based on this, and in all but three of the 'second family' bestiaries that I have seen.

Figs. 47–50. *Initials to the Book of Tobit, with 'swallows'. Compare Pl. 12.*

47. *The bird has a forked tail, but is otherwise not recognisable as a swallow or martin; no nest visible but dung goes to Tobit's eye. Bible illuminated by William of Devon, B.L. MS. Roy. 1D.i, f. 215r. English, 3rd quarter of 13th century.*

48. *Bird more swallow-like; globular nest and no dung. Trinity College Cambridge MS. 0.4.27 (James 1258), f.198v. English, late 13th century.*

49. *A recognisable swallow sits on the rim of its bowl-shaped nest. C.U.L. MS. Add. 6159, f. 218r. English, early 14th century.*

In most the tail is forked, but the red throat is shown in only two, Bodleian Lib. MSS. Bodley 764 (Pl. 17) and Ashmole 1511, which is rather earlier. Most of the birds are, apart from their tails, unrecognisable as swallows, and some are absurd. In B.L. MS.Sloane 3544, for example, there are three fattish short-tailed birds on the ground in long grass. *Hirundo* is in the 'fourth family' bestiary, and in all those of the third; only in C.U.L. MS.Kk.4.25 is there a good example, with a red throat and possibly a red forehead, which has been smudged.

50. *A white bird, not a swallow, on the wall (it is similar to some of the birds in the Creation scene on f. 3v); nest doubtfully visible on left; three white lines of dung extend towards Tobit's eye. Bible of Richard II, B.L. MS. Roy. 1E.ix, f. 126v. English, c. 1410.*

Thrushes

Thrushes are conspicuous by their song, and sometimes by their behaviour, but are for the most part dull in colour, usually brown with much spotting, so that they are not good subjects for decoration and are difficult to recognise if they do occur. Although many of the smaller birds that systematists include with the thrushes, such as the redstart, are highly coloured, of these only the robin is at all familiar to the ordinary man.

There are a few probable blackbirds, for example in the Alphonso Psalter (Pl. 21, Fig. 51) and the Sherborne Missal (p. 385). In the latter, the bird, which is labelled 'throstel cok', has a red beak, and so have the bird illustrating the story of St. Kevin and his blackbird (*merula*) in Giraldus (B.L. MS.Roy.13.B.viii, f.20r), which is not otherwise like a blackbird, and a brown blackbird-like creature in the Pepysian Sketchbook (Pl. 2). The Latin versions of Aristotle describe the bill as *rutilus*, which according to Lewis and Short's dictionary means red, golden red or reddish yellow. Perhaps the artists followed this rather than any knowledge of the bird, or has the colour of the beak actually changed?

There are a few birds that may be song-thrushes, for example in the Alphonso Psalter (Pl. 1), the Bird Psalter (f.85r) and the Holkham Bible Picture Book (Pl. 10), and one good one in a 13th century manuscript at Hereford Cathedral (Pl. 48). A bird in the Gregory *Moralia* at Cambridge (Emmanuel Coll. MS.112, f.50r) might be either a song thrush or a mistle thrush. There is a fieldfare, labelled 'vveldvare', in the Sherborne Missal (p. 392) and a possible candidate in the Bird Psalter (f.85r).

Of the small thrushes, the only one that is at all common in manuscripts is the robin, of which I have counted 16 in 13 manuscripts, although the identification of some of these is doubtful. Artists sometimes applied dabs of red or pink merely for effect, and it is not always possible to be sure whether a picture is intended to be a robin, a chaffinch or a linnet, or nothing in particular. There is an undoubted robin in the Holkham Bible Picture Book (p. 10), and another good one in the Sherborne Missal (p. 382), labelled 'roddoke robertus'.

The nightingale was well-known in the Middle Ages for its song, and was probably

Fig. 51. *Blackbird. Alphonso Psalter, f. 12r (detail of Pl. 21). English, before 1284.*

kept in cages, but it is hard to distinguish from other little brown birds. The most likely representation is in the Bird Psalter (f. 70r). This also has a bird which may be a stonechat (f. 82v), and there is what may be a redstart in the Alphonso Psalter (f. 18v).

The large thrushes are almost completely absent from continental manuscripts, the only ones that I have seen, apart from the Pepysian blackbird already mentioned, being one doubtful blackbird and two doubtful song thrushes. There are several possible robins, especially in French 15th century manuscripts, and a few drawings that may represent nightingales. The spread of the common thrushes from forests into gardens and suburbs is recent, and occurred later on the continent than in Britain.

The only thrush to occur at all commonly in bestiaries is *merula,* the blackbird. It is in the *Aviarium,* and in some copies of the second, third and fourth 'families'. The drawing usually shows a passable black bird, but is sometimes an absurd shape. The bill is yellow in B.L. MS.Sloane 278 and red in Bodleian Lib. MS.Douce 88(ii). A French 'Bestiaire d'Amour' based on Pierre de Beauvais (B.L. MS.Harley 273) has an unrecognisable bird in a cage. The Hofer-Kraus bestiary has a white blackbird, which possibly refers back to Aristotle, who said that *kottuphos* was white in Arcadia.

One 'third family' bestiary, (Westminster MS.22) has *turdus* without a picture. *Luscinia,* the nightingale, is in two 'transitional' bestiaries, many of the second 'family', three of the third and in the fourth 'family'. The illustration is never recognisable, but the bird is sometimes singing; in B.L. MS. Sloane 3544 it is shown singing to three men in bed. In some manuscripts it is duck-like.

Tits

The tits are common, unconspicuously coloured, lively birds, but they are rare in English manuscripts. The blue tit is the most notable, occurring in four, and being for the most part well-drawn. The *Historia Scholastica* (Pl. 35) and the McLean Bible (f.73r) contain good examples, and the Grey-FitzPayn Hours two that are definite but not so good (ff.3r and 45r), while the De Lisle Psalter has two possible candidates (Pl. 27). All these are dated around 1300 or a little earlier. The only great tit of which I am certain is in the Smithfield Decretals (Pl. 35), but there is a bird which probably qualifies in the Bardolf-Vaux Psalter (Lambeth MS.233, f.81v) and another more doubtful one in the Creation medallion of C.U.L. MS. Dd.1.14. These are later than the blue tits, except possibly for those in the De Lisle Psalter, which may overlap with them. On f.55v of the Ormesby Psalter is a bird which is correctly coloured for a coal tit, including the white nape-spot, but it is poorly shaped (Pl. 25). The only other coal tit is discussed under Pl.36, and the Sherborne Missal has also a longtailed tit (Fig. 52).

The tits of French and Flemish manuscripts are quite different. Out of 33 Books of Hours from the 14th and 15th centuries that I have fully examined, nine have great tits, and they are present also in some of which I have seen only odd pages in reproduction, including the Grandes, the Petites and the Brussels, but not the Très Riches, Heures of John Duke of Berry. (The birds of this Duke's magnificent Books of Hours deserve a special study; many of the passing references to them are wrong.) There are also some great tits in other types of French and Flemish manuscripts, but I have seen only two earlier than 1300: B.L. MS.Harley 2449, where there are three, all rather poor, and the 'Somme le Roy' decorated by Honoré (Fig. 56). A French great tit of c.1350 is shown in Pl. 43.

Blue tits are not as common in continental manuscripts as great tits, but much more common than in English; only six of my series of 33 Books of Hours have them. There are three, all rather poor, in the Missal of St. Denys, and two in the Trinity Book of Hours. There are several in the Duke of Berry's Grandes and Brussels Hours. The Rohan Hours have on f.5v a bird in which the

Fig. 52. *Longtailed tit. The Sherborne Missal, p. 386. English, c. 1400.*

artist has conflated a blue tit and a great tit.

I have seen no continental coal or longtailed tits.

Tits do not occur in the bestiaries, except that *la mesenge* is in some versions of Pierre de Beauvais (McCulloch, 1962).

Miscellaneous passerines

There are a few small birds that occur rarely, and some whose identification is doubtful.

The *martinetas* of Giraldus Cambrensis (Pl. 20) are intended to be dippers as well as kingfishers, but they are not recognisable as such.

There is a bird labelled 'larke' in the Sherborne Missal (Fig. 53). It is speckled, and would pass as a lark, but one could not be certain of the identification. Another speckled bird with a slight crest in the Pepysian Sketchbook (f.11v) may also be a skylark.

An Apocalypse at Lambeth (Fig. 54) has a group of animals in a tree consisting of a squirrel, a horned owl, a bird which may be a pigeon, two that are unrecognisable, and one in the very characteristic and unusual attitude of a nuthatch. Its beak is the correct shape, but the back is green instead of blue and the breast red instead of reddish buff. These colours are perhaps near enough to suggest that the artist was trying to reproduce a woodland scene that he had actually witnessed. Nuthatches are among the birds that do mob owls.

The Sherborne Missal has an excellent grey shrike (Pl. 37). A 13th–14th century

MISCELLANEOUS PASSERINES

Diurnale at Sidney Sussex College Cambridge (MS.62; unfoliated) has several birds in outline only except for a little yellow wash that is applied indiscriminately as a primitive kind of shading. Near the middle of the manuscript are three birds that are distinctly shrike-shaped, with beaks that are more or less correct. I cannot, however, be certain that they do represent shrikes. The Hours of Marguerite de Foix have on f.202r a bird that might be a great grey shrike.

Fig. 53. *Lark.* The Sherborne Missal, p. 369. English, c. 1400.

Fig. 54. *Nuthatch? owl, two unidentifiable birds and a squirrel with the beast and the false prophet being thrust into a lake of fire.* Apocalypse (19:20), Lambeth MS. 209, f. 34v. English, 3rd quarter of 13th century.

The hedge sparrow is one of the brown spotted birds that is difficult to distinguish from many others. There may be one in the Alphonso Psalter (Pl. 1), and possibly another in the Bardolf-Vaux Psalter (f.64r), where it is singing. The Fitzwilliam Museum's list claims that there is one in the Bird Psalter (f.145v), but this seems to me to be unrecognisable. It has a slightly cocked-up tail, suggesting a wren.

There is a rather poor starling, labelled 'stare', in the Sherborne Missal (p. 385), and another, rather better, in the Luttrell Psalter (Pl. 34). A French Book of Hours (B.L. MS.Add.29433, f.13v) and the Flemish Trinity Coll. Camb. MS.B.11.22 (f.213r) also contain starling-like birds.

Fair pied wagtails occur twice in the Bird Psalter (Pl.48) and in the Sherborne Missal (p. 371). Three manuscripts of a treatise on surgery by John Arderne (B.L. MS.29301, f.16r, Glasgow University MSS.Hunter 251, f.26r, and Hunter 339, f.69r) contain little sketches of 'wagster' to illustrate the text, but in none is the bird recognisable. According to Vaurie (1971) the Psalter of Bonne of Luxembourg includes three species of wagtail among its many birds.

Warblers are too uniform in colour for any of the brownish birds in the manuscripts to be certainly assigned to them. A brown bird with a black head in the Gregory *Moralia* at Cambridge could be a cock blackcap, but there is too much black on the head, since it comes well below the eye. This manuscript is generally associated in style with the Ormesby Psalter, but the birds give no support to this view. A few French and Italian manuscripts contain warbler-like birds, the best being a possible *Phylloscopus* in B.L. MS.Add.29433 (f. 217r).

The last of this miscellaneous group is the wren, which occurs in at least 11 English manuscripts, including five of the East Anglian Psalters (Pls. 10,11,15,28). Although its colouring is not distinctive, its characteristic short, cocked-up tail is. A few of the 14th and 15th century French and Flemish Books of Hours contain wrens, but they are on the whole not as well-drawn as the English ones (Pls. 43,44,47).

Few of these miscellaneous birds are mentioned in the bestiaries. All those of the third 'family' have *alauda,* the lark. In Westminster MS.22 it is shown flying up from *falco;* in C.U.L. MS.Kk.4.25 it is very small with a peacock's crest; in Fitzwilliam MS.254 it is without the crest; in Bodleian Lib. MS.Douce 88(ii) it is a small brown flying bird, and in Bodleian Lib. MS. e Musaeo 136 it is not illustrated. I cannot agree with McCulloch's statement that the illustrations in all these bestiaries 'resemble one another markedly'; in this instance, for example, the artists of the Westminster and Douce manuscripts seem to have drawn a bird with which they were familiar, while the illustrator of the Cambridge University manuscript had never seen a lark, but knew that it has a crest. The only 'fourth family' bestiary has *regulus,* which perhaps meant the wren, with a nondescript drawing.

CONCLUSIONS

From the foregoing discussion, and from the notes on the Plates, it is possible to make certain generalisations. Birds of one sort or another are present in manuscripts throughout the Middle Ages, with a frequency that varies with place and time. There are fewest in the Romanesque period, roughly the 11th and 12th centuries. Before and during this time there is little attempt at accurate representation. Especially in the earlier years the birds are used, as in the Lindisfarne Gospels (Pl. 4), as a starting-point for a pattern, a form of art that may be found elsewhere in Celtic metalwork and Saxon sculpture. In shape they may be formalised as in the Book of Kells (Figs. 13,14) and colour is usually applied at the artist's whim, as in the rooks of the Oxford Bede manuscript, where the illustrator must have known that they are in fact black, and not the purple, red and green that he made them. Not until the mid-13th century, in Gothic manuscripts, does there appear any attempt at the kind of accurate drawing that might satisfy a modern illustrator; one of the earliest of these is the Trinity Apocalypse (Pl. 13). There is then a sudden flowering of birds as decoration, which reaches its climax in England in the early years of the 14th century (Pls. 24–30), and soon afterwards ceases even more abruptly than it began.

Development on the continent ran a parallel course in some ways but not in others. In the early years there was little comparable to the decorative use of birds in the Lindisfarne Gospels and The Book of Kells, although when they were used they were equally unnatural (Fig. 55). Although birds occur in some of the continental early Gothic manuscripts (Fig. 56), they are rarely in such profusion as in England. At the end of the 14th century they become more frequent, and about a hundred years after the English climax there is a new one, French or perhaps Franco-Flemish, in which birds are as abundant as before. There are, however, differences. The borders containing the birds surround a picture, not a page of text (Pls. 44,45,47), and in the later 15th century become floral rather than leafy. Some of the birds are reasonably well-drawn, but there is a tendency to exaggerate tails and beaks, and the birds are often in unnatural attitudes. The final degeneration comes at the end of the

Fig. 55. *Unrecognisable birds, black, and gold. Moutier-Grandval Bible, B.L. MS. Add. 10546, f. 26r. French, c. 840.*

Fig. 56. *Goldfinch and great tit in scene showing the Seven Virgins watering the trees of the mystic garden. Le Somme le Roy, by Honoré. B.L. MS. Add.*

54180, f. 69r. French, end of 13th century. The background is gilt.

century in such a book as the Hours of Englebert of Nassau, which has two or three birds on nearly every one of its 500 pages. But only 30 or so can be identified and many even of these are inaccurate; for example, six of the nine peacocks have no crest. This is not because the artist could not draw — ff.97v–98r have good copies of peacock feathers — but because he was aiming at something different.

The ornithologist will want to know how far these birds were drawn from nature and how far they were copied from other drawings. The general answer given by art-historians is that they were copied, and it is indeed clear that they sometimes were. The resemblances between some bestiary pairs (Pl. 17) or the Apocalypses of the first 'family' (Figs. 57,58) are so great that some common origin is the only reasonable explanation. But to proceed from this, as is sometimes done, to the implicit rule that nothing is ever drawn for the first time, is unjustified. When a good jay first appears, in the Trinity Apocalypse at some date between 1230 and 1250, the most likely explanation is that the unknown artist (obviously a master craftsman on other grounds) saw a jay, and decided to put it in his picture (Pl. 13). When another jay, different but in its way equally good, occurs in a later manuscript (Fig. 40), it is likely that the second artist also had a real bird in mind or in front of him, even if he also knew the Trinity manuscript.

Fortunately, it is often possible to say with confidence whether a drawing of a bird is taken from nature or from another drawing. There is not space here to detail all the evidence, but it is based on long experience of students and of commercial artists making biological drawings. They make mistakes, both when drawing specimens and in copying, but on the whole they make more in copying. (I do not doubt that meticulous copying, as formerly taught in art schools, is possible; I state what happens in practice.) The reason for this is presumably psychological; the attention that is needed in making a representation of a specimen appears to be greater than that required in simply copying someone else's drawing, and so detail is recorded that is often missed in a copy. This is well shown in such manuscripts as the Bible of William of Devon, the Trinity Book of Hours, and the

Figs. 57–58. *The 'Call of the Birds' in Apocalypses of the first family.*
  57. *Bodleian Library MS. Auct. D.4.17, f. 19v. English, mid-13th century.*
  58. *Rylands Library MS. 19, f. 20v. Flemish, 14th century.*

Missal of St. Denys, each of which has a series (parrots, goldfinches and great tits respectively) which looks as if it consists of copies done by one artist from a model, either his own or someone else's.

There is supporting evidence that artists could have known many of the birds they drew. The crane, peacock, parrot, jay, magpie and goldfinch, six of the commonest, were all kept in captivity, and owls were used as decoys. The use of birds in the decoration of French manuscripts reaches a peak just at the time when the king and great nobles kept big aviaries full of birds, largely the same species – goldfinches, linnets, chaffinches – as appear in the manuscripts that they commissioned, and the birds are often shown flying, as they would be in aviaries; the earlier English birds, drawn at a time when they were kept chiefly in small cages (in which the pictures sometimes show them), are hardly ever seen in flight.

The contrast between the decorative birds of religious and other manuscripts and those of the bestiaries is striking. Many examples have been given above of species that are well known to the ordinary illustrators but unrecognisable in the bestiaries; *graculus* (if this means jay) is one of the most notable. Even when a bird such as the swallow or parrot is more or less correct it is often badly drawn. It seems that the illustrators of bestiaries often ignorantly copied their predecessors, and in some cases tried to follow the text without knowing the birds they were supposed to be drawing.

Copying falls into two classes: the straightforward copying of one manuscript to make another, similar one, and the copying of items in a model-book. Where the text of two or more manuscripts is the same, it may well be that one is copied from another, and if so there is every reason why the pictures should be copied also. But similar texts may be produced by dictation to a group of scribes, and if this practice were followed, the pictures would have to be added later, when they might differ from each other. Some of the illustrations in the Hofer-Kraus bestiary have been pricked through (Ives and Lehmann-Haupt, 1942), showing how multiple copies of outlines were probably produced. The 'families' into which the bestiaries and Apocalypses have been classified are based on similarities of text, and to some extent illustrations within a given 'family' are also similar, but there is nevertheless much freedom, suggesting that an artist was generally permitted to do what he liked, even if he had an illustrated text before him from which to work.

Model-books or pattern books certainly existed, but few survive; Scheller (1963) knew of 31, nearly all of which were later than 1350, and none was indisputably English. If they had been much used for the manuscripts discussed here I should have expected to find more. Much has been made of the Pepysian Sketchbook (which, for reasons given under Plate 2, is almost certainly French or Italian), but it is remarkable that nearly all the comparisons that have been made have been with earlier manuscripts; the gull on f.11v, for example, has been repeatedly compared with the one in the Alphonso Psalter (Pl. 1). So far as this suggests anything it is that, rather than being a formal model-book, to be used by practitioners, the manuscript is a student's sketchbook, and the fact that several of the drawings are of dead bird skins, which do not appear elsewhere, tends to confirm this.

The only good evidence for the use of models is internal. I have already referred to series of degeneration in goldfinches, parrots and great tits, and there are a few cases where the same unusual version of a bird appears in more than one manuscript; there is for instance the same rather odd jay in the Peterborough Psalter (f.48v) and the Ramsey Psalter (New York, Morgan 302, f.76r), which on other grounds Sandler (1974) has assigned to the same painter, and another pair of jays, different from the last but similar to each other, in the Peterborough Psalters at Brussels (f.14r) and Corpus Christi College, Cambridge (f.189r), which she allots to different workshops. There are peacocks with similar unusual and imaginary crests in the Bible of William of Devon (f.1r), an Apocalypse at Lambeth (MS.75, f.45v), and a Bible (Lambeth MS.89, f.4). These examples are discussed more fully in Yapp (1979). Five somewhat similar little owls are dealt with under Pl. 39 (cf. Fig. 59). Most medieval bird drawings are, however, unique, and there is every reason to think that the good ones at least were made from living specimens.

I have written here only of the birds, and I am well aware that the usual art-historical approach, based largely on details of the drawing of the human figure and its costume, sometimes points to rather different conclusions; here is a problem for the future to

Fig. 59. *Peacock and little owl. Book of Hours, B.L. MS. Harley 2887, f. 29r. English, c. 1460. Compare Pl. 39.*

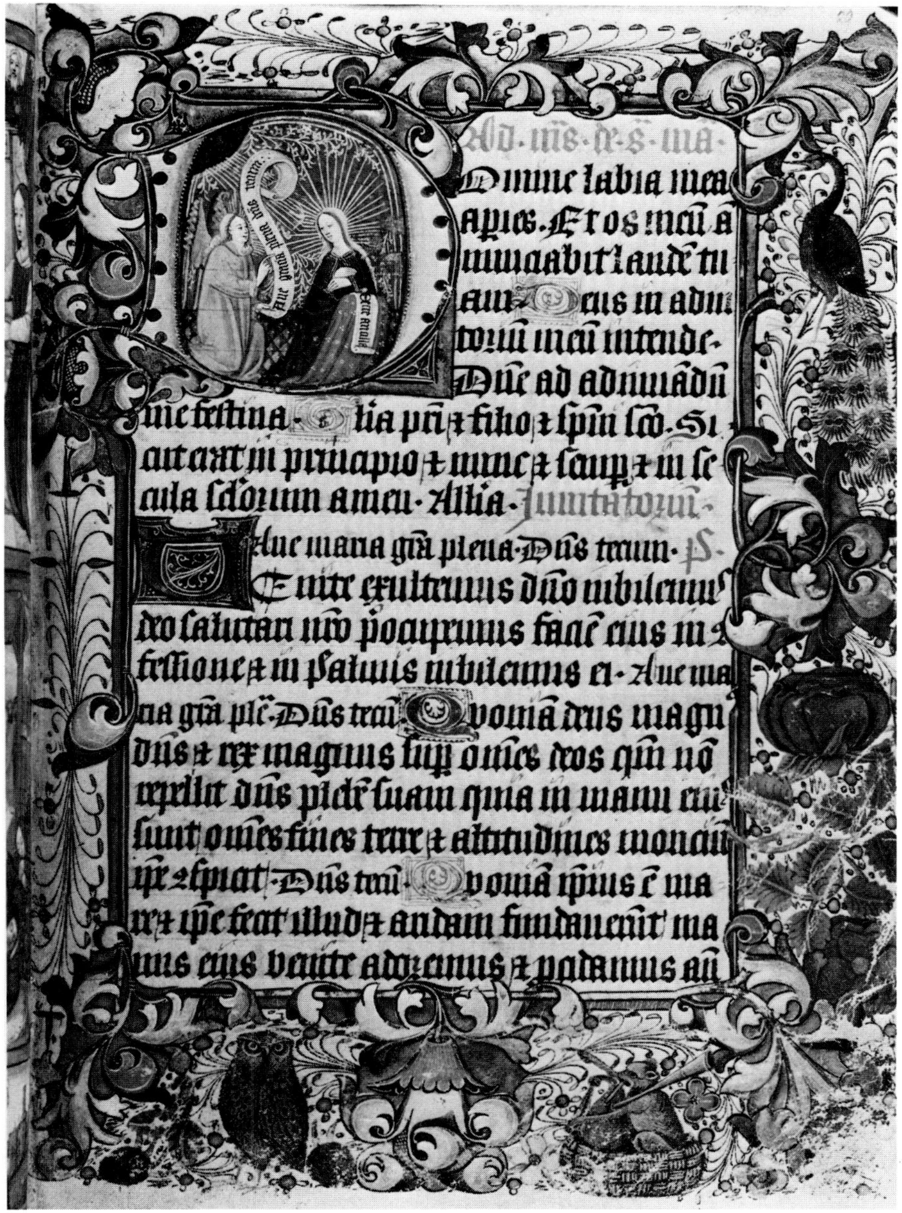

solve. Pächt (1943) stressed the influence of Giotto and his followers on the East Anglian manuscripts of the early 14th century, but it must be remembered that the birds on f.11r of the Alphonso Psalter (Pl. 1) were drawn when Giotto was a boy. The birds in a mural sometimes attributed to him in the Upper Church at Assisi, are half obliterated, but according to Howe (1912) appear to have included goldfinch, chaffinch, jay, turtle dove, thrush, quail, green and great spotted woodpeckers, jackdaw, great tit, hawfinch and robin; this list must be treated with caution, but it is in length and most of its species truly East Anglian. Whoever the artist was, the work is apparently at least ten years later than the Alphonso Psalter. In a short visit to the Arena Chapel at Padua I could see no birds in the murals of c.1304–13, said to be the earliest work which can certainly be ascribed to Giotto. Martindale (1967) writes of the Alphonso Psalter (Pls. 1,21,22,23) and the Douce Apocalypse (Bodleian Lib. MS.Douce 180; its birds are unidentifiable), 'both these manuscripts show that, in taste, the court in London was following the court in Paris fairly closely', and I would not dispute this; however, the Alphonso Psalter shows in its birds both a taste and an accomplishment that Paris did not achieve until a hundred years later, and then in a different, and, from an ornithological point of view, inferior way. They did not always order these matters better in France.

Fig. 60. *Hawk and duck. Decoration on purse-lid from Sutton Hoo Treasure. British Museum, 7th century. Compare Pl. 22.*

COLOUR PLATES

PLATE 1

The Alphonso (or Tenison) Psalter. B.L. MS. Add. 24686, f. 11r. English, before 1284.

I have placed this first because, although it is by no means the latest, it is probably, from an ornithological point of view, the best page in any medieval manuscript. I do not think such good pictures were drawn again until the nineteenth century.

The birds hardly need identification. Starting top left and going clockwise they are: woodpigeon, hen and cock bullfinch; a grey bird with a spotted breast; a goldfinch; a green woodpecker; a kingfisher; a gull; a bird rather like the spotted one above; a crane. If those that I have named are compared with skins or accurate modern drawings, it will be seen that the colours are correct in almost every detail; there is a little too much red on the goldfinch's head, and the blue on the kingfisher's cheek does not meet that on the back. Other details are correct – the knob on the pigeon's beak and the spiky tail of the woodpecker. The jizz (the general attitude and impression) is fairly good, and all except the crane are drawn more or less to scale, which is unusual.

It is always difficult to know how much reliance to place on small details of colour that the artist could easily have got wrong, but in view of his general accuracy on this page the yellowish legs and absence of the red splash from the bill suggest that the gull was carefully drawn from a common gull; compare Pl. 16, Fig. 37.

The lower spotted bird has the jizz of a song thrush, which it probably is; the upper is more like a hedge sparrow in jizz, but might be another thrush.

Other folios of this manuscript are shown in Pls. 21–23.

Beatus vir qui non
abijt in consilio im-
piorum: et in uia pec-
catorum non stetit.
7 in cathedra pestilen-
cie non sedit.

Sed in lege domini
uoluntas eius: 7 in
lege eius meditabit
die ac nocte.

Et erit tanquam lignum quod plantatum
est secus decursus aquarum: quod fructum suum dabit in tempore suo.
Et folium eius non defluet: et omnia quecumq.
faciet prosperabuntur.
Non sic impii non sic: sed tanquam puluis
quem proicit uentus a facie terre.
Ideo non resurgunt impii in iudicio neq. peccatores in consilio iustorum.
Quoniam nouit dominus uiam iustorum: et i-
ter impiorum peribit.

Quare fremuerunt gentes: et populi meditati sunt inania.
Astiterunt reges terre 7 principes conuenerunt

PLATE 2

Pepysian Sketchbook or Monk's Drawbook. Magdalene College Cambridge
MS. Pepys 1916, f. 12v. Probably Italian, c. 1400.

Four leaves of this manuscript are covered with coloured drawings of birds and mythical animals, and the rest with various sketches in ink. The folio shown has a grey partridge, a kingfisher, a probable blackbird (dark brown for black and red for the beak occur elsewhere), perhaps a pigeon and a duck, a water rail with its distinctive zigzag markings, and a cock house sparrow. There is another water rail on f. 13r of the *De arte venandi cum avibus;* in England it is a shy and skulking bird, but on the continent it is often seen walking in meadows as moorhens do here. On f. 10v are two red-legged partridges (fig. 16) and on ff. 11r and 11v two different birds which, if they are identifiable at all, are blackheaded buntings or ortolans. This constellation of continental species suggests strongly that the manuscript was probably French or Italian in origin. James (1925) claimed that it was English, his only reason being that birds were characteristic of English manuscripts; however, in 1400, the date that he gave it on the basis of the armour on other pages, this was not the case. His view has been generally accepted, as has his comparison of its birds to those of The Sherborne Missal (Pls. 36 and 37), to which they bear no resemblance. Pächt (1950) and Scheller (1963) saw Lombard features in some of the other figures, but did not draw the simple conclusion that the manuscript is Italian. The birds are, indeed, fairly close in style to those in the Sketchbook of Giovaninno de Grassi (Bergamo Biblioteca Communale, MS. Delta vii.14), which is certainly Lombard and of the late 14th century.

Altogether some 33 species are shown, of which 27 are specifically identifiable, the most interesting being a herring gull on f. 11v. Many of James's identifications are incorrect (Yapp 1979). There are also, from the bestiary, a pelican, a phoenix and (in black only) an ostrich.

83

PLATE 3

The Lindisfarne Gospels. B.L. MS. Cotton Nero D.iv, f. 209v. English, c. 700

This Gospel Book was written by Eadfrith, monk and later Bishop of Lindisfarne in Northumbria, shortly before 700, and was probably illuminated by him also. The decoration has been discussed in great detail by Bruce-Mitford, in Kendrick et al. (1960). Each gospel has a portrait of the evangelist with his symbol and a 'carpet page' in which beasts, birds and geometrical designs cover the whole folio so as to form an elaborate cross; and in all four, the beginning of the first chapter is written in large letters with decoration similar to that of the carpet pages. Matthew has an extra decorated page for 1:18, and the Preface has a carpet page and illuminated beginning. There are also some small decorated capitals here and there.

Plate 3 shows the eagle of St. John, one of the best known and most persistent of the avian symbols; it is still in use at St. John's College Cambridge. Eadfrith has found it difficult to render a flying bird correctly, which is not surprising – a flying dove by G. F. Watts in the Faringdon Collection at Buscott House is almost as awkward. The plumage is good, so good that it must have been done with a bird, possibly even a golden eagle, at hand. The distinction between breast feathers, under wing-coverts and primaries is correct, and the line dividing the small feathers of the neck, which are not individually shown, from the breast is nearly in the right place. The detail of the feathers, each with a rachis and two rows of barbs (especially good in the coverts) could hardly have been invented. The beak is more or less correct, but the eye is too far forward. This eagle is in contrast to most Johnian eagles, which are merely conventional birds with hooked beaks.

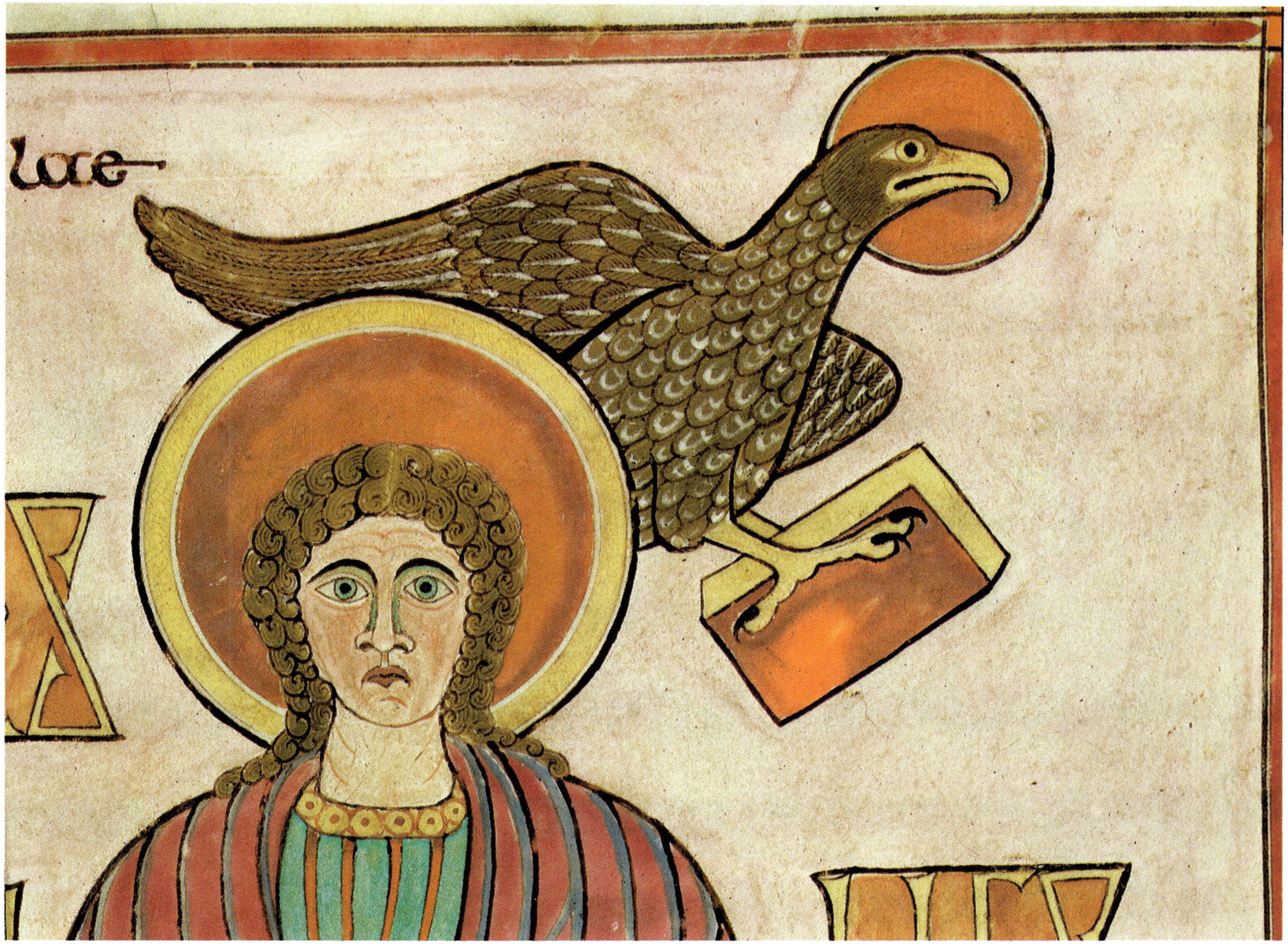

PLATE 4

The Lindisfarne Gospels. B.L. MS. Cotton Nero D.iv, f. 2v.

The birds in the decoration are said by Bruce-Mitford to be 516 in number, and to be all of the same type. The second statement needs qualification. There are certain common features: a somewhat elongated pear-shaped body; a large head with a longish beak hooked at the tip; long legs and toes; a tail that is clearly unnatural, since it becomes involved in the interlace; and sometimes a crest that also takes part in the interlace. Eagle Clarke, who examined them for Baldwin Brown (1921), said they were cormorants, while J. D. MacDonald, advising Bruce-Mitford, thought they were based on birds of prey.

The birds shown here differ from those on other folios, and give a clue to what the artist had in mind. Under the usual tail, shown (as it is elsewhere) as a double outline that becomes entangled with the similar double outline of the neck of the next bird, is an ordinary tail. The only possible bird that apparently has two tails is the peacock, in which an ordinary tail, which can be seen from the side when the bird runs (Fig. 10), lies beneath the elongated tail coverts that are erected in display. The birds on f. 2v are more brilliantly coloured than those on other pages. I conclude that the Lindisfarne birds are based on peacocks, with simplification on most folios. On f. 211r are two birds with highly coloured double tails, neither of which takes part in the interlace. Some birds on f. 139r are similar to this but are uncoloured and have feathered necks (Fig. 8). Elsewhere on this page there are mistakes in the interlace, and here only there is a distinct cat's head; I suggest that this page was not done by Eadfrith.

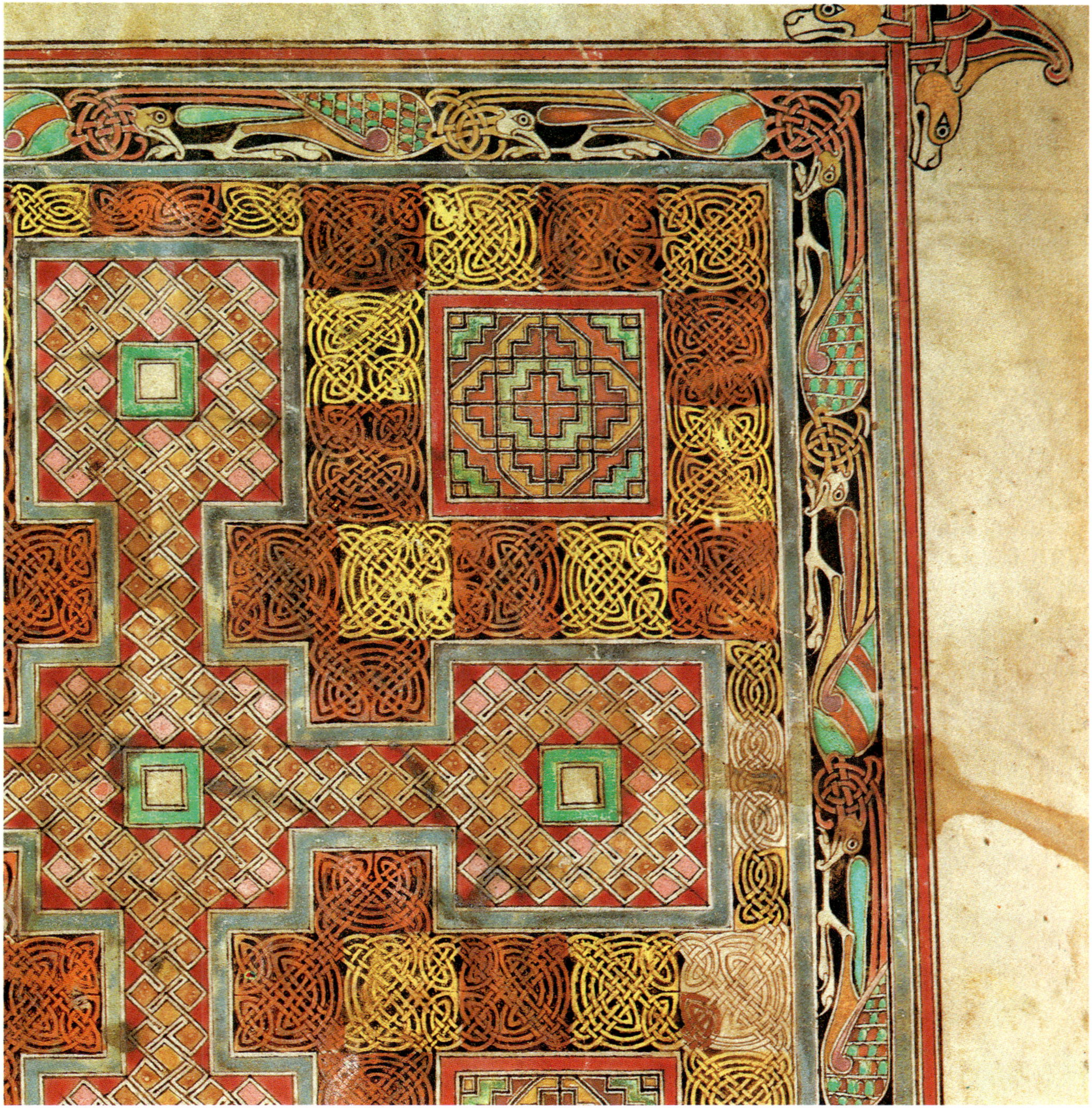

PLATE 5

The Book of Kells. Trinity College Dublin MS. A.I.6, f. 32v. English or Irish ('Insular'), late 8th century.

The Book of Kells belongs to the same family of decorated gospel-books as The Lindisfarne Gospels, but is about 100 years later. Its decoration is richer, more baroque, and further from the tradition of Celtic and Saxon metalwork on which that of Lindisfarne is based.

The folio shown here presents a problem. Once held to be a displaced portrait of either Mark or Luke (the book has been mutilated and rebound more than once), it has more recently been believed to be a portrait of Christ. Henry (1974), who agrees with this view, nevertheless gives several reasons against it and only one in its favour: the birds under the arch are symbolic of Christ because they are peacocks. But are they? The bright colours and longish neck and tail may suggest this, but that is all. The beak is that of an eagle, the feet appear to have curved claws, and there is no attempt to show eyes in the tail. So far the evidence is fairly evenly balanced, but one needs to compare these with other birds, especially those which, because of their context, must be eagles of St. John. On ff. 1v, 2r, 5r (Fig. 13), 27v, 129v, and 290v (Fig. 14) these have circular patterns in the tail or wings or both that look like eyes, and in ff. 27v, 129v and 290v the tails are fairly long and expanded at the end. The type of neck seen on f. 290v is almost exactly the same as that of birds on f. 32v.

I conclude that the artist knew little of the eagle except that it has a hooked beak, but that, knowing that the living creatures seen by St. John were 'full of eyes before and behind', he used the peacock as his model. The birds of f. 32v may be peacocks or they may be eagles, but they give no clue to the identity of the subject of the portrait.

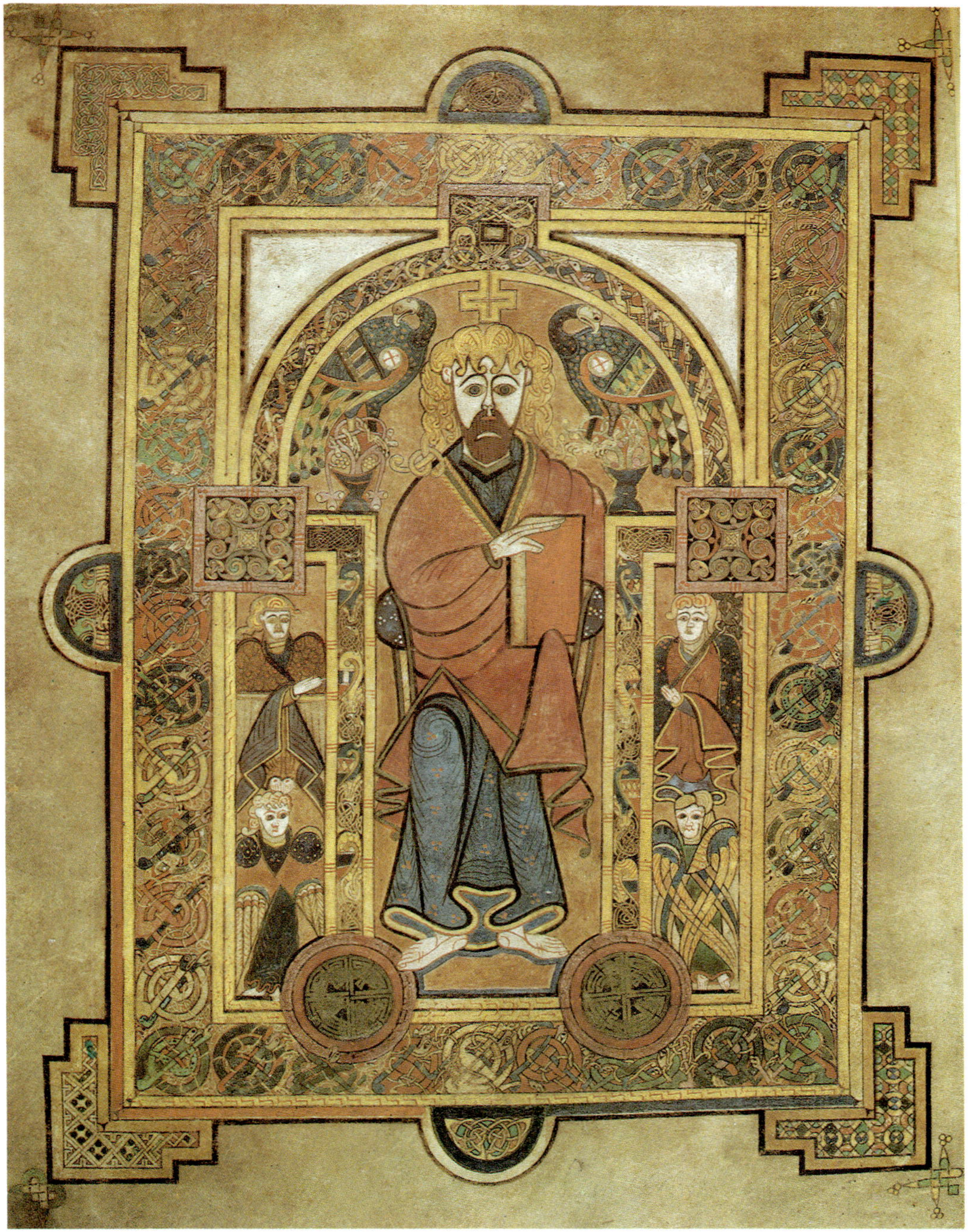

PLATE 6

Golden Gospels. B.L. MS. Harley 2788, f. 12v. German, c. 800.

This book is one of several manuscripts that take their name from being written largely in gold. They were illuminated in the Rhineland, probably in Trier (Trèves), and belong to a school associated with Charlemagne and a lady named Ada, perhaps his sister; they are roughly contemporary with the Book of Kells. Charlemagne had his seat at Aachen, and encouraged scholars from Italy, England and the East, so that influences from all these places have been found in the books produced at his court. However that may be, the title-page, shown here, has birds that are much more natural than those in any Insular manuscript that has survived from that time; no one could be in any doubt of the identity of the peacocks and the farmyard cocks. The smaller birds are not so clear; one would expect the females of the two species, and this is what they may be. The possible peahens at the top have double tails, but the heads look more like those of pheasants. The lower pair, if they are intended to be farmyard hens, have been influenced in shape, and perhaps in colouring, by the red-legged partridge.

The peacocks are, as is nearly always the case, somewhat impressionistic; there are five pin-shaped feathers on the head instead of the correct two dozen, and there are only six large 'eyes' on the tail; compare Pl. 10.

Other folios of the book have more peacocks and farmyard cocks, and there are several eagles, none of which is as good as that in the Lindisfarne Gospels shown in Pl. 3. There are other birds based on ducks, and on cranes, herons or passerine birds, but they are not specifically identifiable.

HAEC SUNT
EVANGELIA
NUMERO QUATUOR
SEC MATTHEUM
SEC MARCUM
SEC LUCAM
SEC IOHANNEM

PLATE 7

Echternach Gospels. B.L. MS. Harley 2821, f. 11v. Luxembourg, mid-11th century.

Most of the early gospel-books have at their beginning a series of lists of the corresponding passages in the different gospels, which had been drawn up by Eusebius, Bishop of Caesarea in Palestine. These Eusebian canon-tables came by convention to be arranged under a series of arches or pediments, as if written in panels on the end of a building. In the Lindisfarne Gospels the columns and arches on some folios are filled with birds very similar to those in Plate 4 (though without double tails), and in the Book of Kells the eagle and other evangelist symbols appear in various combinations at the top (Fig. 13). More usually birds, and very occasionally mammals, are shown standing or walking up the top of the arch outside the frame. The earliest canon-tables known, in the Rabula Gospels (see Cecchelli et al., 1959) which were written in Northern Iraq in the 5th or 6th century, have peacocks, chukar partridges, guinea fowl, ducks, parrots, a wood pigeon and a swallow, and other manuscripts have in addition grey partridges, pheasants, fowls, a bird that may be a bustard, herons, storks, cranes, an owl, magpies and indeterminate passerines. The commonest are birds that are eaten, and the most frequent is the peacock (Fig. 9), which occurs in 19 out of 35 sets of canon-tables that I have seen (mostly in reproduction). Western manuscripts are much poorer in their range of species than eastern.

The plate is of a canon-table from a gospel-book made at Echternach (now in Luxembourg) in the mid-11th century. It shows two good cranes. Other canon-tables in the book have peacocks, unrecognisable passerines, and a possible pigeon, as well as dogs and men.

MATH	LUC	IOH
CANON	TERTIUS	IN QUO III
ii	xiii	i
iii	xiiii	iii
iiii	xiiii	cc
v	vi	ii
vii	vi	xxv
lviiii	lxii	cxvi
lxiii	lxv	xxxvii
xc	lviii	cxviii
xcvii	lviii	cxxxviii
cxiii	cxviii	cxlvii
cx	cxviii	xxx
cxi	cxvii	cxiii
cxii	cxviii	lxxxvi
cxii	cxviii	xliiii
cxv	cxviii	lxx
cxi	cxviii	viii
cxii	cxiiii	lxxv
cxii	cxviii	xc
cxii	cxviii	cliii
cxii	cxviii	cxl
cxlvi	xcii	xlvii

EXPLIC CANON TERCIUS

PLATE 8

Aelfric's Metrical Paraphrase of the Pentateuch and the Book of Joshua. B.L. MS. Cotton Claud.B.iv, f. 3v. English, Canterbury, second quarter of 11th century.

There were some early copies of complete or partial texts of the Bible, but they did not become common until much later than the Insular Gospels. According to Tristram (1873) there are about 40 Hebrew words in the Bible that are translated by birds' names, although the meaning of many is doubtful. Few of them appear in illustrations, the artists having preferred to use scenes, such as the creation and the naming of the animals by Adam, where the text says simply 'birds' or 'fowls of the air' (*aves* or *volucres* in Latin), so that they could choose what species they like.

The present work is a paraphrase in Anglo-saxon written in the early 11th century by a monk called Aelfric for the benefit of those (including many clergy) who could read but did not know Latin. The plate shows the creation of birds. The best that can be said of it is that the artist has tried to show a variety of species. Standing in the foreground is a cock, the only one that suggests that the illustrator knew what he was drawing. To the right the blue bird is probably copied from a drawing of a crane (the red crown is missing), and to the left the white one is perhaps a swan. One of the other standing birds and one of those flying have slightly hooked beaks, and might be hawks or eagles, while the other flying birds might be based on crows or ravens.

The picture of Adam naming the animals (f. 6r) has a similar selection of birds, as do three of the ark (ff. 14r, 15r, 15v), but these include a recognisable raven and dove.

þæt ƿn· ⁊ ða fugelaſ beon gemænifylde ofer eorðan· ⁊ða ƿær geƿorden æfen· ⁊merigen fefifta dæg·

ꝺꝺ cƿæð eac ƿpilce lade ſeo ƿorld forð cuce nytena æu hƿam cynne· ⁊ ſcryo cunde cyn· ⁊ deor æfter heora

PLATE 9

Bible of Robert de Bello. B.L. MS. Burney 3, f. 5v. English, Canterbury, early 12th century.

Many Bibles of the later Middle Ages begin the Book of Genesis with a great bar-initial I (for 'In principio', 'In the beginning') which runs the full height of the page and is filled with medallions showing scenes from the book. In the Bible of Robert de Bello, which was made at Canterbury between 1224 and 1253, the fifth medallion down shows the creation of beasts, birds and fishes (Fig. 12). An owl, a cock and a swan can be recognised, and there are four other birds. In the lowest medallion a conventional dove representing the Holy Spirit is between the Father and the Son, and to the right of this a white dove returns to Noah in the ark, while a raven pecks at a corpse below.

The birds in roundels of this sort are necessarily small and are seldom identifiable. Nevertheless the illuminator has usually tried to show a range of species by varying the shapes and colours. In a few it is possible to guess that he may have had a particular sort of bird in mind, for example a woodcock and a crane in Bodleian Library MS. Auct. D.3.2, f. 1r (English, end of 13th century). In Eton College MS. 177, f. 1v, where six similar roundels have been enlarged to fill a whole page as a picture preliminary to an Apocalypse, an eagle, a crane and a goose are recognisable. This manuscript is English, or possibly French, of the 13th century.

In no two Bibles that I have seen is the number, the colouring or the arrangement of the birds alike. The scene is the same, but the detailed drawing is original. The beasts are often in a different roundel, and it is noteworthy that they are usually the lion plus common domestic species (cf. Pl. 10).

celum et terram. Terra autem erat inanis et uacua et tenebre erant sup faciem abyssi. et sps dni ferebatur sup aquas. Dixitque deus. fiat lux. et facta est lux. et uidit deus lucem quod esset bona. et diuisit lucem ac tenebras. Appellauitque lucem diem et tenebras noctem factumque est uespe et mane dies unus. Dixit quoque deus. fiat firmamentum in medio aquarum. et diuidat aquas ab aquis. et fecit deus firmamentum diuisitque aquas que erant sup firmamentum ab his que erant sub firmamento. et factum est ita. Uocauitque firmamentum deus celum. et factum est uespe et mane dies scds. Dixit uero deus. Congregentur aque que sub celo sunt in locum unum. et appareat arida. factumque est ita. et uocauit ds aridam terram. congregationesque aquarum appellauit maria. Et uidit deus quod esset bonum et ait. Germinet terra herbam uirentem et facientem semen et lignum pomiferum faciens fructum iuxta genus suum. cuius semen in semetipso sit sup terram. et factum est ita. Et protulit terra herbam uirentem et afferentem semen iuxta genus suum. lignumque faciens fructum et habens unumquodque sementem secundum speciem suam. Et uidit deus quod esset bonum et factum est uespe et mane dies tercius. Dixit autem deus. fiant luminaria in firmamento celi ut diuidant diem ac noctem et sint in signa et tempora et dies et annos. ut luceant in firmamento celi et illuminent terram. et factum est ita. fecitque deus duo magna luminaria. luminare mai ut preesset diei et luminare min ut preesset nocti. et stellas. et posuit eas in firmamento celi ut lucerent sup terram. et pcessent diei ac nocti. et diuiderent lucem ac tenebras. Et uidit deus quod esset bonum. et factum est uespe et mane dies quartus. Dixit ds. producant aque reptile aie uiuentis et uolatile sup terram. sub firmamento celi. Creauitque deus cete grandia et omnem animam

PLATE 10

The Holkham Bible Picture Book. B.L. MS. Add. 47682, f. 2v. English, early 14th century.

The birds, although here as in the earlier Bibles used only to illustrate a story, are highly decorative, and resemble many of those that in contemporary psalters simply enliven the page. Those in the Creation in this plate are the kind with which the artist might have been familiar in garden or countryside. They are: a peacock; a horned owl, a probable bullfinch; perhaps a song thrush; two that are unrecognisable; a chough; a probable swallow; a goldfinch; a probable kite; a magpie; an unrecognisable flying blue bird; a raptor attacking a smaller bird; another that is unrecognisable; a robin; and at the bottom a duck, a swan, a lapwing and a crane.

The 'eyes' on the peacock's tail, although too few in number, are well coloured and correctly orientated, with the indentation in the dark centre towards the body. The flying thrush shows ten separated primaries, the correct number. The owl is conventional, and suggests copying from a bestiary rather than from nature.

The chough is interesting. Except that the body is brownish (as is that of the raven that Noah releases from the ark on f. 8r), the representation is good. But choughs are cliff-nesters, and there are no suitable cliffs in London or East Anglia, which are the two areas claimed on indirect evidence as possible places of origin of the manuscript. A Canterbury artist might have seen choughs, since there is some evidence that they nested on the cliffs of Dover in the 17th century. Another explanation would be that choughs nested on buildings such as Norwich Cathedral; this is possible but seems to me to be less likely. Hassall (1954), many of whose identifications are incorrect, calls this a blackbird. In addition to the details that are correct for a chough but not for a blackbird, I should have expected a blackbird in this scene to be singing, as are the other identifiable songbirds (goldfinch, robin, wren).

Omnipotent deu li puissant. En l'eyr fesoit oisels volaunt. Arbres diverses
fruiz portaunt. Acens q estoient auenaunz. De tere fist creitre erbes e flu-
res. De queux les mires fount lurs cures. Bestes sure tere: en ewe peison.
E ren ne est sauns lur nom. Car pur lui tut est fet. Ceel e tere e quant q est.
Cum il le pensoit e le voust. Bien tot fu fet ceo dist lescrit. Rien ne fist de
sa mesure fors home e femme ceo sacez certein. Tutes choses il fesoit flurir e
crestre e il le fesoit pur home servir.

PLATE 11

The Holkham Bible Picture Book. B.L. MS. Add. 47682.

A. f. 3v (part). On this page God forbids Adam and Eve to eat of the Tree of Knowledge, shown as an apple tree. The bird in the middle that looks like a hawk is in fact a conventional pelican, feeding its young with blood from its breast. Immediately on its left a wren sings in a pear tree, and beyond that in another apple tree there is a rather poor robin whose tail appears to have been influenced by the wren. On the other side are a bird which is presumably intended to be a bullfinch in what looks like a guelder rose, and a poor goldfinch in a cherry tree. The goldfinch and perhaps the wren look as if they might have been copied from the same models as those in f. 2v.

B. f. 10r (part). This is the top portion of a diagrammatic descent of Christ from Jesse. On the top branches of the tree, vine on the left, oak on the right, are a parrot, a peacock, an owl and a goldfinch. The parrot's head and back are blue, which is not correct. The peacock's 'eyes' are too large and too few, but correctly orientated. The owl and the goldfinch appear to be the same birds as before.

Hassall (1954) makes much of the symbolism of these species, but to do so he relies in part on a 15th century translation of *lucina* as goldfinch. This is an obvious error, since in other vocabularies the word means nightingale; it is not the only error in the manuscript, from which the vocabulary is printed by Wright (1884). All except the parrot occur elsewhere in the Holkham Bible Picture Book in contexts where they cannot have the symbolism ascribed to them here, so I see no need to regard them as anything but decoration.

A

co mmundement. Tot iras uerrefeirent. Deux ne estoit q un ton al
lee. Ke le defens deux ne fu brifee. co on g̃it tor adã il tefoit. Caunt en certuage

B

PLATE 12

Swallows in the Book of Tobit
A. Sidney Sussex College Cambridge MS. Delta 5.11 (James 96), f. 157v. Anglo-French, c. 1300.
B. Bodleian Library MS. Auct.D.1.17, f. 143v. French? Mid-13th century.

In English Bibles the Book of Tobit is relegated to the Apocrypha, but in the Vulgate it is placed among the historical books of the Old Testament. It recounts the story of Tobit, a Jewish captive in Nineveh. Chapter 2 relates that while he slept under the wall of his house, birds dropped warm dung into his eyes and blinded him. Both the Revised Version and the New English Bible call the birds 'sparrows', but the Vulgate has *hirundinum,* and refers to their nesting; obviously the house martin is the most likely species.

The first word of the book in the Vulgate is 'Tobias', and many medieval Bibles begin it with a large capital T (called an historiated initial) in which this scene is illustrated within the outline of the letter. Tobit lies in bed, usually watched by one or more men, and a bird above flies up to its nest. Two examples are shown in the Plate. A is one of the best. The bird, though tiny, is a fair representation of a swallow, and the nest, with three young, is that of a house martin. B has a similar bird, even smaller, but here the nest is tubular, so that, if not imaginary (which seems unlikely) it is that of a red-rumped swallow. This species is found in the Middle East and sometimes nests on houses, but it is known only as a rare straggler in France and Britain. The artist must therefore have seen it in the Mediterranean or further east.

The manuscript is usually said to be French, but bears some resemblance to those known to have been illuminated by William of Devon, for example B.L. MS. Roy. 1D.i, with which it shares parrots and cranes (Fig. 32). The Tobit scene of this Bible is shown in Fig. 47; it obviously differs considerably from that of Pl. 12B. The Oxford manuscript needs reconsideration.

Other examples of Tobit and his swallows are shown in Figs. 48–50. Each is individual, with little detailed resemblance to any of the others. It there was copying, it was very free.

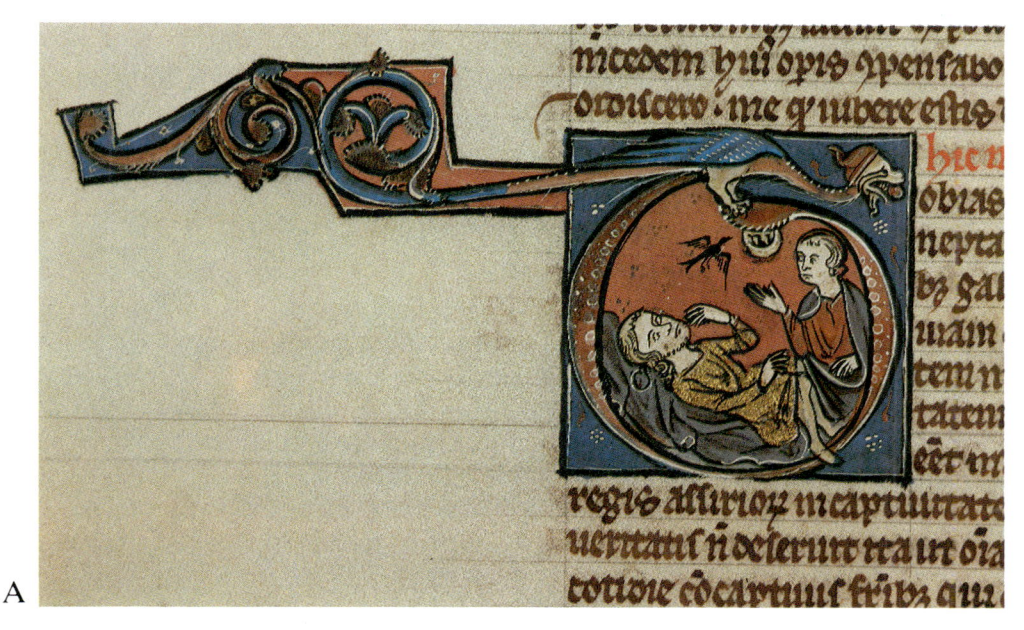

A

B

PLATE 13

Apocalypse Commentary of Berengaudus. Trinity College Cambridge MS.R.16.2. A, f. 23r, B, f. 20v. English, mid-13th century.

In about the middle of the 13th century, illustrated Apocalypses became common, and continued so to the end of the Middle Ages. Nearly 100 examples, most of them English, are known (James 1927 and 1931). The scene with birds most commonly shown is that of 19:17–18; the English of the Authorised Version follows the Vulgate almost word for word: 'and I saw an angel standing in the sun; and he cried with a loud voice, saying to all the fowls [*volucres*] that fly in the midst of heaven, Come and gather yourselves together ... that ye may eat the flesh of kings, and ... of horses, and ... of all men.' Plate 13A shows this depicted in the Trinity Apocalypse, the date of which, to judge by the costume, seems most likely to be a little before 1250. The flying bird is possibly a crane, and a magpie and an unhorned owl sit in the trees. These are birds from the bestiary, and the drawing of them is of about the same standard as that seen in some of the better contemporary bestiaries. Six of the other birds are unrecognisable, and are probably not intended to represent anything in particular, but the one with the blue bar in the wing is clearly meant to be a jay. Plate 13B shows f. 20v of the manuscript, illustrating the Fall of Babylon (18:2); the jay here is much better, and looks as if it might have been drawn from life, one of the earliest examples of this practice for birds other than those kept for the table. There is written evidence that jays were kept in cages during the Middle Ages.

The whole manuscript has been sumptuously reproduced (Brieger 1967).

A

B

pcchurs ki sunt auenir en la fin del munde. P la espere deuine esipnur. P la uerge de fer: le ewangile. P le pressur u psaye parole de la passiun nostre seignur est signifie la crux iku est. Mes le pressur signifie ici le liu de peines u les mauueis serrunt de botz.

E io vi un aungele astaunt en le solail. e il cria od en celestiel pprenseie. E ple ciel nus poum entendre sein graunt vois disaunt a tuz les oseaus ke volent te eglise. Les seins volent ple ciel. pur co k il auaunt

PLATE 14

Apocalypse Commentary of Alexander of Bremen. Cambridge University Library MS. Mm.v.31, f.140r. ?Saxon, 13th century.

This unusual Apocalypse raises several problems. It includes the commentary of Friar Alexander, usually described as of Bremen, though sometimes, incorrectly, of Hales, which was probably written about 1242. Each character is shown with two heads, one that of the person mentioned, the other that of whom he is the type. In the 'Call of the Birds', shown here, the angel's companion is Arnoldus, Patriarch of Jerusalem. The script dates the manuscript to about the middle of the 13th century, and according to James (1909) looks English, but because the commentary was by a German, the manuscript has been assumed to be so also.

The birds are mostly recognisable, and all but one are labelled with Latin names. The owl-like bird on the right is called *hosgriniu'*, a word that I have found nowhere else. With the exception of this, all the names occur in most 'transitional' and later bestiaries. They are, going clockwise: *accipiter* (hawk), *passer* (house sparrow), *corvus* (raven), *aquila* (eagle), *picus* (woodpecker), *pica* (magpie), *grus* (crane), *cygn'* (swan), *cyconia* (stork), *ardea* (heron), *anse'* (two geese). At the bottom right is an unlabelled owl. The drawings somewhat resemble in style those of bestiaries, but are on the whole better and more accurate. The artist has distinguished the three long-legged species — crane, stork and heron — reasonably well, though not all the details are correct. *Picus,* here an unmistakeable green woodpecker (except that it has a superfluous crest), is not normally illustrated in bestiaries.

The long and miscellaneous list of birds in this early Apocalypse completely disproves Klingender's assertion (1971) that there is a progression in the representation of this scene from appropriate carrion-eaters to the ordinary birds of the countryside, caused by confusion with pictures of St. Francis preaching to the birds.

Angelus stans in sole. id est in ipo
erat arnoldus predicator egregi.

Arnold?

venite et congregamini ad cenam magnam dei. ut manducetis carnes regum

aues signant fideles
in altum uolantes.

coruus
aquila
asser
acipiter
halcuinus
pica
columba
grus
pius
anser
ciconia
ardea
cygnus

140

XIX

PLATE 15

Apocalypse with Figures. B.L. MS. Roy. 19 B.xv, f. 37v. English, early 14th century.

This is a later version of the 'Call of the Birds', of about 1325; it has been associated by scholars with the East Anglian School (cf. Pls. 24–30). Apart from the page shown it has few birds, unlike the Trinity Apocalypse, which has swans, geese, a peacock and a partridge, as well as the species already noticed.

The quality of the birds varies. In what looks like a palm tree are (at the top) a wren; a blue and pale green bird; a magpie, with no white in the wing and a long forked tail; a bullfinch, poorly coloured and of rather doubtful sex; an unrecognisable black and white bird; a jay; and another bullfinch, of slightly better colour but still of doubtful sex. The blue and green bird has a large beak, and might be intended for a kingfisher, but it is greenish-white where it should be red; perhaps the artist suffered from the congenital eye-defect called Daltonism, in which red and green look the same. The big black and white bird has the pattern of a black stork, but the jizz is wrong, and this species is so rare in western Europe that such an interpretation would seem very unlikely.

Below the tree are: what appears to be a white heron; a parrot with divided tail; an excellent woodcock, showing well the barred head; and a good crane. In 1544 Turner (Evans 1903) said that he had seen white herons amongst the grey in heronries; they must have been commoner then than now.

ou ceo signifie je sui bon fiz de ceinte Eglise qe sont aussi come la robe
dont il est vestu. crient fermement qe il est deux & homme.

Jeo vi un angel esteaunt en le solail & cria a grant voiz & dit a toutz
les oiseaus qi volent par mi le ciel. venez & assembles vous a la

PLATE 16

Apocalypse. New College Oxford MS. 65, f. 73v. English, late 13th century.

This Apocalypse in French prose, has, like some others, separate illustrations for the 'Call' and for the 'Feast' of the birds. On f. 73r two crows, an owl and three nondescript hawks stand before an angel with outstretched arms, while another hawk and a magpie fly towards him. On the next page, shown here, birds are feeding on the corpses, represented in great detail. There are a crow, a conventional hawk, and (beneath the grey horse) a thrush-shaped bird with colouring that fits no European species. Then there is a herring gull, correct in almost every detail, including the orange splash on the mandible; it should be compared with the common gull of the Alphonso Psalter (Pl. 1).

This manuscript has been dated to the latter part of the 13th century, but little seems to be known about it. The herring gull must have been drawn from life – perhaps from an incident on the seashore – and f. 73v looks as if it was the work of a much better artist that that of f. 73r.

I have seen 48 manuscript Apocalypses, and three more in reproduction. One of the most striking things about them is that the pictures of this scene and the 'Call', which are nearly always illustrated, either separately or conflated, are nearly all unique; the idea may have been conventional, but, as with Tobit's swallows, the execution was original. The exceptions are the four manuscripts of James's first 'family' – B.N. MS. fr. 403, New York MS. Morgan 524, Bodleian Library MS. Auct.D.4.17 (Fig. 57) and Rylands MS. lat.19 (Fig. 58); even in these, the birds are different in number and disposition. Lincoln College MS. 16 (Fig. 40) is similar enough to B.L. MS. Roy. 19 B.xv, (Pl. 15), both in the general arrangement and the birds present (including the rather unusual woodcock), to suggest that the artist of one had seen the other.

111

PLATE 17

The bestiary swallow (*hirundo*).
A. B.L. MS. Harley 4751, f. 52v. English, late 12th century.
B. Bodleian Library MS. Bodley 764, f. 81v. Second quarter of 13th century.

These two 'second family' bestiaries are so similar, both in text and pictures, that all scholars agree that either they were copied from the same prototype, or, more probably, the later Bodley manuscript was directly copied from the other. There are some differences of detail in the pictures shown here – for example, in the disposition of the timbers of the building – and the gable-end in the Bodley manuscript has fewer planks and is asymmetrical. The Harley manuscript has only one bird on the right and shows six young in the nest, while Bodley 764 has two adult birds but does not certainly show any nestlings. The most interesting difference is that, in Bodley, one of the birds on the left clearly shows the red throat, a characteristic feature of the swallow that could only have been added from personal observation. There is literary evidence that in the Middle Ages swallows nested within the houses of the poor, with their glass-less windows, so that they would have been easy to observe. The possibility that a copyist might know better than his master, and so correct his model, has usually been ignored and has sometimes been denied, but this example shows that correction did happen. (The parrot also in the Oxford manuscript has accurate details that are absent from the other.)

As in most of the Tobit initials (Pl. 12), although the birds are swallows the nests are those of house martins. These are possibly the only illustrations of *hirundo* in bestiaries that are reasonably natural. In all the others that I have seen the bird may have a forked tail, but is otherwise not much like a swallow.

A

B

PLATE 18

Bestiary. B.L. MS. Roy. 12 C.xix. English, c. 1187.
A. f. 38r, *aquila*.   B. f. 38v, *vultur*.

    This plate illustrates the fact that bestiary pictures, whatever their artistic merits, seldom reveal the same accuracy as many of those in other manuscripts. *Aquila*, the eagle, is here shown in three of the activities mentioned in the text: catching fish, flying toward the sun until it is scorched, and plunging into a fountain to cool itself. The first of these suggests that the account was originally based either on the white-tailed eagle or on the osprey, but no one could tell that from the pictures.

    The vultures here, as in other bestiaries, hardly differ from the eagles, such details as the slightly less hooked beak and the red outlines to the feathers being merely accidental, and not repeated elsewhere; I have known an expert on manuscripts think that a picture of a vulture, which was on the preceding page to the text, was merely a repeat of that of the eagle, which came just before.

    To be fair, one should remember in comparing this bestiary with other manuscripts that in the 12th century there were no good drawings of birds. But this is one of the bestiaries with the best illustrations as well as one of the earliest of the English ones, and the birds seldom improve as time goes on.

    The background of both drawings is burnished gold.

A

B

PLATE 19

Le Livre des Propriétez des choses. B.L. MS. Roy. 15 E.iii, f. 11r. Flemish, 1482.

This is a version of *De Proprietatibus rerum* by Bartholomew de Glanville, which was composed in the 13th century. It was one of the three great encyclopaedias of natural history of the Middle Ages. This manuscript, written at Bruges by Jehan de Ries, is of the French translation made by J. Corbechon, and is one of the few copies of the encyclopaedias that have any illustrations. The plate shows the frontispiece. The border does not differ in style from other manuscripts illuminated in Flanders in the second half of the 15th century. Of the seven birds that it contains only a peacock and peahen are real birds; the one with the blue crest can hardly be a blue jay, since the Cabots did not discover the coast of North America until 15 years later. The birds in the central picture are, on the other hand, mostly natural species that were probably present in or around Bruges at that time, although certainly not in a cluster like this. A white stork, a magpie, a swan, a crane (its head brown not red as it should be), a cock and hen, a hoody crow and a carrion crow or rook facing it, are immediately identifiable. Some of the others may be guessed. But legend has crept in. The owl on the cliff is a bestiary bird not a natural one, and above it a phoenix arises from the flames; in the tree just to the right a mythical pelican pecks her breast. The crane carries a snake, although in the bestiaries it is the stork that does this.

There are more fantastic birds on f. 67v, and on f. 200r a good cock bullfinch and a good goldfinch.

Cy commence le douzieme
livre des proprietes des choses
ou il traicte premierement
des oyseaulx en general. et
apres en particulier.

Puis que nous a-
uons ou premier
volume determi-
ne de lair et des
impressions qui y sont en-
tendues. maintenant ap-
partient et nous reste de

dire aucune chose de ce qui
affiert a son mouuement.
A celle fin que la maiestu-
de et puissance du createur
soit en eulx loee et magni-
fiee comme es autres creatures. A l'ornement
de lair donques appartient
les oyseaulx et toutes choses
qui volent. sicomme dist
bede le venerable. Et pour
ce a l'ayde de dieu nous en
dirons ung pou de chose

PLATE 20

A. Giraldus Cambrensis, Topographica Hibernica. B.L. MS. Roy. 13 B.viii, f. 9v. English, early 13th century.   B. Bestiary. B.L. MS. Harley 4751, f. 37v. English, late 12th century.

These pictures show how an illustrator sometimes interpreted the text in his own way, so that it is not always necessary to look for prototypes in Byzantium or elsewhere. Giraldus lived in the second half of the 12th century and into the 13th, dying perhaps in 1220. His histories include an account of a visit to Ireland. There he saw birds, of which his account (in translation) reads:

> There are little birds called martins, smaller than a blackbird, rare here as elsewhere, and living by streams; short like a quail and plunging into the water on to tiny fishes, on which they feed. Although otherwise they retain their nature in all things, they vary in colour only. For here, with their white underparts and black back they are becoming unlike their kind, while in other places, with their red breast and reddish beak and feet and indeed with their back and wings gleaming bright green like a parrot or peacock, they are strikingly beautiful.

Obviously he was conflating the dipper and the kingfisher, which is not surprising, since he was describing them for the first time. Plate 20A shows a rather poor attempt to illustrate this. Plate 20B is from a bestiary that appears to be earlier than the Giraldus manuscript. The editor has taken the passage about martins almost word for word from Giraldus, and his illustrator has interpreted it quite successfully.

Plate 20A also shows *ciconia*, the stork. The artist is, however, muddled; the tail and brown head suggest a crane, and the crest a heron.

A

B

do cuicutas rapit & dispgu.   Martinete.

Sunt in hybernia auicule quas martineta uocant merula

PLATE 21

The Alphonso Psalter. B.L. MS. Add. 24686, f. 12.

This page shows a crane made into a grotesque in the characteristic East Anglian Gothic manner; the fluffy secondaries have become the face of a bearded man and the bird has been given webbed feet. At the bottom is a good cock blackbird with a yellow beak and orange iris (Fig. 51).

The well-drawn red deer stag should also be noted; this species is less common in manuscripts than the fallow.

We do not know where the Alphonso Psalter was produced, but its style, especially in relation to the birds (of which there are probably 17 species), is that of the slightly later manuscripts written and illuminated in East Anglia (Pls. 24–30). It was intended for the wedding of Alphonso, son of Edward I, but only the first quire, ff. 11–18, was completed before 1284, when the young prince died. It appears to have been done under Dominican influence, and, for this reason only, the London house of Blackfriars has been suggested as its place of origin. There is also an indication in the calendar of a connection with Bury St. Edmunds, which would bring it close to the places of origin of the East Anglian manuscripts of the next century (Hutchinson 1974). Even in the 13th century the kingfisher, and more particularly the capercaillie (Pl. 23), seem unlikely to have been familiar to urban artists. I see no reason why the commission for the work should not have been given to a rural workshop.

Domine quid multiplicati sunt qui tribulant me: multi insurgunt aduersu me.
Multi dicunt anime mee: non est salus ipsi
in deo eius.
Tu autem domine susceptor meus es: gloria
mea et exaltans caput meum.
Voce mea ad dominum clamaui: et exaudiuit
me de monte sancto suo.
Ego dormiui et soporatus sum: et exsurrexi qui-
a dominus suscepit me.
Non timebo milia populi circumdantis me: ex-
surge domine saluum me fac deus meus.
Quoniam tu percussisti omnes aduersantes
michi sine causa: dentes peccatorum contriuisti.
Domini est salus: et super populum tuum be-
nedictio tua.

Cum inuocarem exaudiuit me deus ius-
ticie mee: in tribulatione dilatasti michi.
Miserere mei: et exaudi orationem meam.
Filii hominum usquequo graui corde: ut quid
diligitis uanitatem et queritis mendacium.
Et scitote quoniam mirificauit dominus
sanctum suum: dominus exaudiet me cum cla-
mauero ad eum.

PLATE 22

The Alphonso Psalter. B.L. MS. Add. 24686, f. 14v; detail.

This scene of a hawk attacking a duck occurs in a number of medieval manuscripts, including the Vatican copy of the *De arte Venandi cum avibus* (f. 69r), and a late French work on Falconry by Guillaume Tardif (Glasgow University Library MS. Hunter 269), where not only a duck but a pheasant, a partridge and a heron are shown as prey. (These hawks are rather nondescript, but others in the manuscript are fair goshawks.) The scene is also used more than once as decoration, among English manuscripts for example in Queen Mary's Psalter (B.L. MS. Roy. 2 B.vii, f. 151r) and a Book of Hours (B.L. MS. Harl. 6563, f. 76r), both of the early 14th century, and in an early 15th century psalter (C.U.L. MS. Dd.12.67, f. 103v). The Harley Hours have a hawk attacking a hare or rabbit as well (f. 7r). A falcon and a duck occur together on ff. 11v and 12r of the Pepysian Sketchbook, and this has sometimes been taken as evidence that the scene was commonly copied, as at times perhaps it was. But when hawking was a popular sport among the rich it must have been a common enough sight for artists to have used it without having seen a picture of it elsewhere. It occurs, in a somewhat stylised form, on a purse-lid in the Sutton Hoo treasure, which was out of view from its burial in the 7th century until its rediscovery in 1939 (Fig. 60).

The duck in the plate is clearly a drake mallard, although the colouring is not entirely accurate. The raptor is a fair representation of a goshawk (the bird most commonly used for flying at ducks), with no moustachial stripe. It is not, as it is sometimes called, a peregrine.

alfissime

PLATE 23

The Alphonso Psalter. B.L. MS. Add. 24686, f. 18r.

I cannot see any connection between the drolleries here — a man in chain mail stabbing a griffin and a crow or raven about to peck at the wounds presumably inflicted on the knight's horse by the animal — and the latter part of Psalm 14 and beginning of Psalm 15 that they accompany. The shaggy neck of the bird may indicate that it is meant to be a raven and not a crow. A rather poor magpie, with not enough white and a tail incorrectly forked at the tip, is above left. The fat bird at the bottom right is fairly close to a cock capercaillie; the red on the face (though there is too much of it) and the shaggy head especially suggest this (Fig. 17). If it is not this, it must be imaginary, but imaginary birds are usually less bird-like in jizz than this, and there are no others in the manuscript.

Capercaillies are birds of coniferous forests; they became extinct in Scotland in the 18th century, and there is no direct evidence for their occurrence at any time in England except as Pleistocene fossils. They were presumably present when the natural woodland was Scotch fir, but Ray (1678) says firmly that they were then found 'nowhere in England'. Most if not all coniferous forests disappeared from England long before historic times, but some foresters think that pockets did persist right through until the 18th century when planting on a large scale began. On the continent the capercaillie lives in mixed deciduous and coniferous forests as well as in pure tracts of the latter, and there might have been enough firs in East Anglia in the 14th century for it to have survived.

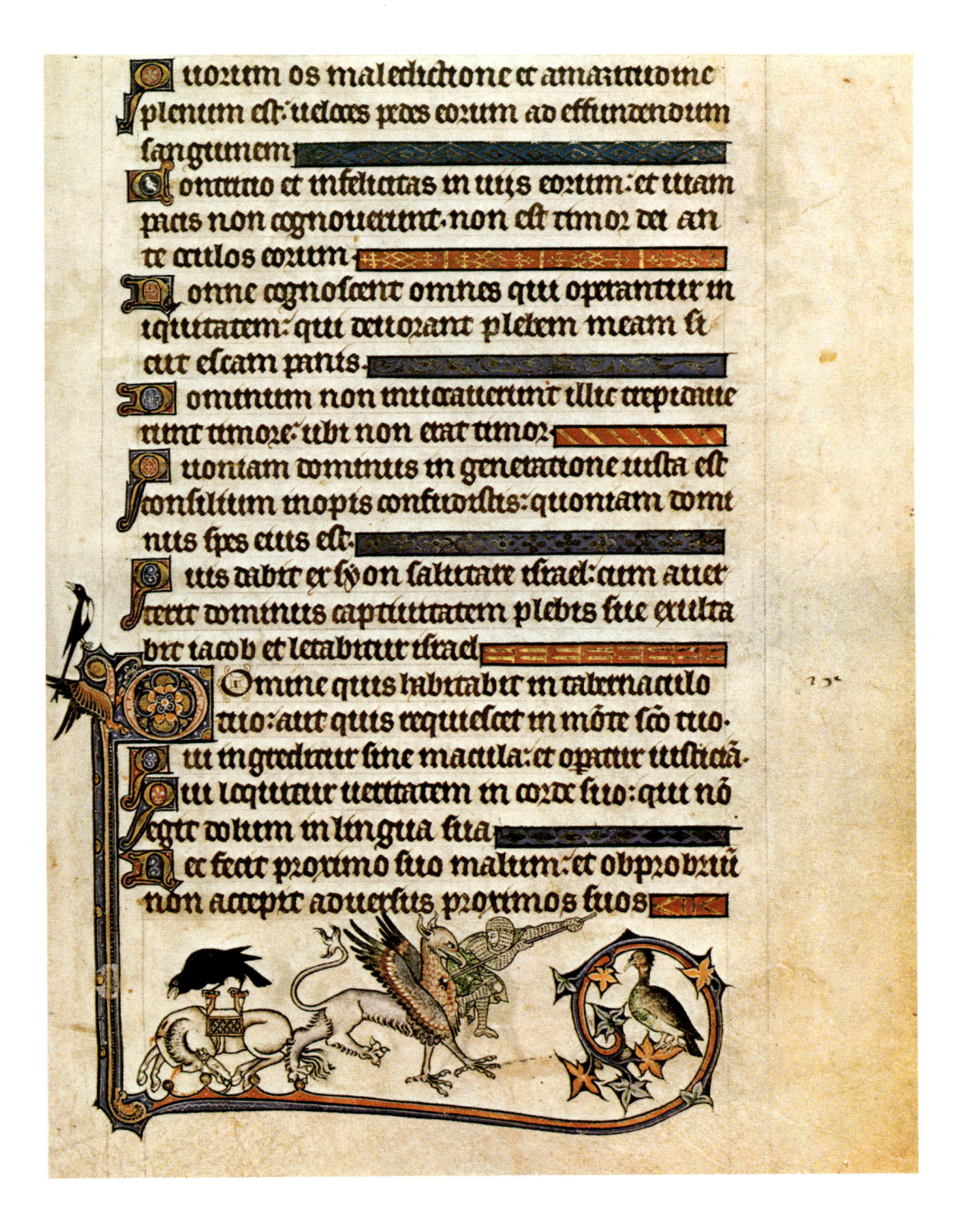

mortem os maledictione et amaritudine
plenum est: ueloces pedes eorum ad effundendum
sanguinem.

Contritio et infelicitas in uiis eorum: et uiam
pacis non cognouerunt. non est timor dei an
te oculos eorum.

Nonne cognoscent omnes qui operantur in
iniquitatem: qui deuorant plebem meam si
cut escam panis.

Dominum non inuocauerunt illic trepidaue
runt timore: ubi non erat timor.

Quoniam dominus in generatione iusta est
consilium inopis confudistis: quoniam domi
nus spes eius est.

Quis dabit ex syon salutare israel: cum auer
terit dominus captiuitatem plebis sue exulta
bit iacob et letabitur israel.

Domine quis habitabit in tabernaculo
tuo: aut quis requiescet in monte sancto tuo.

Qui ingreditur sine macula: et operatur iustitiam.

Qui loquitur ueritatem in corde suo: qui non
egit dolum in lingua sua.

Nec fecit proximo suo malum: et obprobrium
non accepit aduersus proximos suos.

PLATE 24

The Ormesby Psalter. Bodleian Library MS. Douce 366, f. 38r.
English, first quarter of 14th century.

This is one of the earlier of a group of manuscripts, mainly psalters, produced in what is broadly called East Anglia, many of which are decorated with birds. It was given to the Cathedral of Norwich in about 1325 by Robert of Ormesby.

The plate shows Ps. 26 (Dominus illuminatio mea), a folio which is said to have been added to the main part of the Psalter in about 1310. On the right are a robin with good jizz and a goldfinch that lacks any yellow, with a magpie below. The white wing-bar is somewhat misplaced; the light green cheek-patch may be an attempt to show the irridescent sheen on the black feathers. In a roundel is a tawny owl, in a good posture, looking backward. At bottom left is a well-drawn goshawk or sparrow hawk, feeding on what appears to be the leg of a bird. Just above the big initial D is a bird whose tail suggests a wren; but it has a blue and white bar in the wing which shows that it is probably intended to be a jay, the tail having been accommodated to fit the space available.

The Ormesby Psalter has other animals besides birds. At the top of the plate are a snail (*Helix aspersa*) and a small tortoiseshell butterfly (*Aglais urticae*), and at the bottom an excellent red squirrel (*Sciurus vulgaris*) eating a nut. On f. 147v (Pl. 26) three ladybirds (probably *Coccinella septempunctata*) in the right-hand margin alternate with three imaginary insects. Except that each has 10 legs, the ladybirds are fairly well drawn.

am tuam famulis tuis supplicib; ⁊ fac
nos in tua ueritate deuotos. ut actibz nr̃is
si innocentia restitutis. liberari mereamur
ab impiis. per.

ominus illuminatio
mea et salus mea: quẽ
timebo.
D̃ns protector uite mee:
a quo trepidabo
um appropiant super me nocentes: ut e
dant carnes meas.
ui tribulant me inimici mei: ipsi infir
mati sunt ⁊ ceciderunt.
i consistant aduersum me castra: non ti
mebit cor meum.
i exurgat aduersum me prelium: in hoc
ego sperabo.
nam petii a domino hanc requiram: ut i

PLATE 25

The Ormesby Psalter. Bodleian Library MS. Douce 366, f. 55v.

This page, Ps. 38 (Dixi custodiam), which also is said to have been added to the Psalter in about 1310, but to be by a different artist from that of f. 38, has only one bird, at the bottom left. Every detail of the pattern — white cheeks, nape-spot and wing-bar, with dark crown, throat, primaries and tail — is correct for the coal tit, for which it must be intended, in spite of the more finch-like shape. It is the only certain coal tit that I have seen in any manuscript (but see the notes on Pl. 36).

The picture at the base illustrates the bestiary story that a unicorn (*unicornis*) can be caught only when it rests its head in the lap of a virgin.

There are several other birds in the manuscript, but most of them are more or less caricatured. On f. 89r (Ps. 68, Salvum me fac) there is fairly good green woodpecker, and there is another drawing, possibly intended to represent this bird, on f. 109r (Ps. 80, Exultate Deo).

It is remarkable that, although there are at least a dozen English psalters from around 1300 with well-drawn birds in the decoration, in no two of them is the assortment of species the same. The most lavishly illustrated psalm is usually Ps. 1 (Beatus vir), but even this is not a fixed rule; the Ormesby Psalter has two Beatus pages, but neither has any birds except for a conventional dove in one of them (f. 9v). The subjects illustrated within the initial, on the other hand, are much more sterotyped. (Most of them are listed in Sandler (1974), pp. 98–99.)

The flowers in these medieval manuscripts, though often confidently given names in the books, are in truth seldom identifiable. Here, however, there are on the left good corn flowers (*Centaurea cyanus*) and on the right buds of a vetch of indeterminate species. The leaves belong to neither of these.

ti deploramus: valeamus evincere in
sultationes adversantium vitiorum. per

ixi custodiam vias
meas: ut non delin
quam in lingua me
a. Posui ori meo cu
stodiam: cum con
sisteret adversum me.
Obmutui z humiliatus sum z silui a bo
nis: z dolor meus renouatus est.
Concaluit cor meum intra me: z in me
ditatione mea exardescet ignis.
Locutus sum in lingua mea: notum fac
michi domine finem meum.
Et numerum dierum meorum qui est:
ut sciam quid desit michi.
Ecce mensurabiles posuisti dies meos:
z substantia mea tamquam nichilum ante te.

PLATE 26

The Ormesby Psalter. Bodleian Library MS. Douce 366, f. 147v

This page, Ps. 109 (Dixit Dominus) is said to be by the same artist as f. 55v, and so by a different one from f. 38, but the birds do not support this. In particular, the jay with the wren-like tail in the roundel on the left is the same bird as that on f. 38. The blue and white patch on the wing is damaged in the manuscript, but clearly present. The other birds filling the corners round the initial are finches. The two on the right have a good deal of green, on crown, back and wings, and the upper one has a slightly forked tail. All these characters suggest that they are greenfinches. The wing of the upper bird, presumably drawn from a dead specimen, is well done. There is one primary feather too many (a very common type of mistake, still often made by artists and even by zoologists), but their disposition, with the length gradually decreasing from the second visible one (strictly the third, since the first is minute and hidden) is good. There is even some suggestion of emargination of the webs. This wing should be compared with the impressionistic raised wings of French birds in Pls. 42, 43 and 46B. I am not sure of the identity of the fourth bird; it has something of a juvenile look, and might be a hawfinch, a bird that I have seen elsewhere only in the Grey-FitzPayn Hours (Pl. 32) and perhaps the Peterborough Psalter (Pl. 30).

This page is (like many others) also notable for its drolleries, one of which, at the top of the page, combines a joke with a bird. An owl, which could well be a young tawny, is riding, sitting backward, on a hare, pursued by a greyhound and a monkey wearing falconers' gloves, waving a lure and (presumably) a piece of meat. Some of these drolleries have been said to be derived from Italy, but we have seen a monkey engaged in hawking in an English Apocalypse of the mid-13th century (Fig. 20).

cet a persequentibus animam meam.
Ute obsecrationis dne deus. qui
maledictioni subiacere dignat'
es. ut nos a maledicto legis erueres. 7 fa
ceres nobiscum misediam: ppc nom tuu
digneris nos 7 a psequentibz uictis. et a
malorum obtrectationibz liberare. per.

ixit dominus
domino meo: sede adextris meis.

PLATE 27

The De Lisle (or Arundel) Psalter. B.L. MS. Arundel 83, f. 14r. English, c. 1310.

Experts agree that the first part of this book, shown here, is early 14th century, and in a development of the East Anglian style.

The group of birds at the bottom of the page is interesting in that it shows an actual scene from the countryside (Fig. 21). The man in a pink gown crouching under a bush is holding an owl, and so must be a bird-catcher. The use of an owl as a decoy is referred to in the English poem 'The Owl and the Nightingale' of the early 13th century, and is described by Ray (1678). The birds assembled to mob the owl are difficult to identify. On the right is a magpie, and vertically above its rump is a goldfinch in a hawthorn; two birds with blue in their wings on each side of this are probably jays; there is another, better one in the oak on the left. In the middle the bird with a black head is probably a cock bullfinch, and his mate faces him, half hidden in the hawthorn; behind him is a goldfinch and a bird with a blue head, perhaps a blue tit although not much like it. The pole on which the cock bullfinch and one goldfinch sit is presumably part of the net in which the birds are to be caught, or it may be covered with bird-lime.

A similar scene, in which the clap-net is much more clearly drawn, the owl sits on a stake and appears to be stuffed, and five little birds fly around, is on f. 38v of the Très Riches Heures of the Duke of Berry of c. 1415. Longnon and Cazelles (1969) miss the point by describing it as a cleric 'chasing birds with a ladder'. Almost exactly the same scene as in the Très Riches Heures, but without the owl and with a monkey instead of a man holding the net, is on f. 32v of the Metz Pontifical of about the same date as this psalter.

Non auferetur: amen. a

Seruite. ame. a Ps fidei. ae.

Beatus uir qui non abijt in
consilio impioy z in uia
peccatoy non stetit: et in
cathedra pestilencie n sedit.
Sed in lege dni uolunta
eius: z in lege eius medi
tabitur die ac nocte.
Et erit tamquam lignum
qd plantatum est secus de
cursus aquarum: qd fructum
suum dabit in tempore suo.
Et folium eius non deflu

et: z omnia quecumque faci
et semp prosperabuntur.
Non sic impij non sic: sed ta
quam pluus quem proicit
uentus a facie terre.
Ideo non resurgunt impi
in iudicio: neque peccatores in con̅sil
io iustorum: z it ipioy pibit.
uare fremuerunt gentes:
z populi meditati sunt ian̅ia
stiterunt reges tre z prin
cipes conuenerunt in unu:
aduersus dn̅m z aduersus xpm e.
Dirumpamus uincla eoy:
z piciamus a nobis iugu ipoy.
Qui habitat in cel' irridebit
eos: z dn̅s subsanabit eos.
Tunc loquetur ad eos in ira
sua. z in furore suo conturbabit eos
go autem constitutus
sum rex ab eo super syon mon
tem scm eius predicans preceptum eius
Dn̅s dixit ad me filius meus
es tu: ego hodie genui te.
Postula a me z dabo tibi
gentes hereditatem tuam: et

PLATE 28

The Saint Omer Psalter. B.L. MS. Add. 39810 (formerly Yates Thompson 14), f. 7r.
English, c. 1330.

This is one of the most elaborate schemes illustrating the first Psalm (called the Beatus page from its first word) in any East Anglian Psalter. The birds are so small as to be difficult to identify; some refer to the biblical scenes in the roundels, some are pure decoration (Fig. 2).

Top right is a peacock in its pride; its solid crest, in gold, is unique. Next below comes a raven — which has no doubt come from the ark on the left — pecking at the throat of a horse. At the base, just above and to the right of the expulsion of Adam and Eve from Eden, is another raven or crow in a tree, and in the middle of the base, above Adam and Eve holding fig-leaves in front of them, is a pair of birds that look like stock-doves. Vertically below them is a group of four birds with little colour. They are unrecognisable, but one has a red head and so may be intended for a goldfinch. To the left of these a short-winged hawk is attacking a brown bird that has a red webbed foot and so is probably a duck. Below are a crane and a swan. Vertically above this group is a magpie facing a bird with a cocked-up tail suggesting a wren, although it is nearly as large as the magpie.

This, together with the lost Douai Psalter, is sometimes said to be the finest production of the East Anglian school. In general decoration perhaps it is, but in its birds, it is inferior to some of the earlier ones.

eatus uir
qui non a
but in con
silio impi
orum. ⁊ in
uia peccato
rum
non stetit:
⁊ in cathe
dra pestilencie non sedit.
Sed in lege domini uoluntas eius: et in
lege eius meditabitur die ac nocte.
Et erit tamquam lignum quod planta
tum est secus decursus aquarum: quod fruc
tum suum dabit in tempore suo.
Et folium eius non defluet: et omnia q
cumque faciet prosperabuntur.
Non sic impii non sic: sed tamquam pul
uis quem proicit uentus a facie terre.

PLATE 29

Peterborough Psalter. Brussels, Bibliothèque Royale MS. 9961–9962, f. 14
English, c. 1300–1318.

This Psalter, which was given to the papal nuncio by the Abbot of Peterborough, for whose Abbey it was written, in 1318, is usually described as 'East Anglian', but Sandler, who has discussed it in great detail (1974), has separated it and a few others as 'Fenland'. Its lavish use of birds in the decoration of the important psalms is shared, however, not with the works that she associates with it, which contain hardly any, but with the De Lisle, Ormesby, and St. Omer Psalters, which she leaves as East Anglian. Altogether it has at least 20 species, slightly more than the earlier Alphonso Psalter (Pls. 1, 21–23) and the later Luttrell Psalter (Pl. 34).

In the initial B of this plate, which shows Psalm 1, David playing his harp is watched by a robin and a crane. Above, Reynard the Fox carries a cock with a long tail. To the right of them in the upper border are a conventional owl, a goldfinch, and either another robin or, since it has streaked wings, perhaps a linnet. In the lozenge below is a goshawk or sparrowhawk, flanked by a jay and a bird of which I can make nothing. The next lozenge has a corvid of some sort, completely out of scale, on the back of a sheep or goat. It has a light iris, and so is probably intended for a jackdaw, a species which does indeed often sit on the backs of animals in this way. It is flanked by two more corvids, possibly again jackdaws. The lowest lozenge has a crane, with good fluffy secondaries and a red crown. Below are a black bird with red legs which must be a chough, and a bird with a crest like a hoopoe, which it can hardly be. Five small birds – possibly blackbirds, since some of them have red beaks – sing in the trees above the hounds in the lower border. In the left-hand margin a young man is apparently attempting to catch a white bird that has a beak of a duck, goose or swan.

As a line-filler in the left-hand column of text is a fairly well-drawn drake or mallard.

Beatus vir qui non abiit in consilio impiorum et in via peccatorum non stetit: et in cathedra pestilentie non sedit. Sed in lege domini voluntas eius: et in lege eius meditabitur die ac nocte. Et erit tamquam lignum quod plantatum est secus decursus aquarum: quod fructum suum dabit in tempore suo. Et folium eius non defluet: et omnia quecumque faciet prosperabuntur. Non sic impii non sic: sed tamquam pulvis quem proicit ventus a facie terre. Ideo non resurgunt impii in iudicio: neque peccatores in consilio iustorum. Quoniam novit dominus viam iustorum: et iter impiorum peribit.

Quare fremuerunt gentes: et populi meditati sunt inania? Astiterunt reges terre: et principes convenerunt in unum: adversus dominum: et adversus xpm eius. Dirumpamus vincula eorum: et proiciamus a nobis iugum ipsorum. Qui habitat in celis irridebit eos: et dominus subsannabit eos. Tunc loquetur ad eos in ira sua: et in furore suo conturbabit eos. Ego autem constitutus sum rex ab eo super syon montem sanctum eius: predicans preceptum eius. Dominus dixit ad me: filius meus es tu: ego hodie genui te. Postula a me: et dabo tibi gentes hereditatem tuam

PLATE 30

Peterborough Psalter. Brussels, Bibliothèque Royale MS. 9961–9962, f. 26.

This is Psalm 26 (Dominus illuminatio mea). In the right-hand border are a jay, a probable robin, and a bird about which I am doubtful. The closest species would seem to be the hawfinch, and if this drawing had occurred in the Grey-Fitzpayn Hours I should have said that it was a degenerate version of the better one of f. 29 of that work (Pl. 32). In view of this, the similarity between the hunting scenes at the bottom of the previous plate and of Pl. 32 should be noted; smaller resemblances than this have been held by some art-historians to establish the identity of artists. Below the doubtful hawfinch is a long-necked, long-legged, long-billed bird with a crest, which, if it is anything in particular, is a heron. At the base of the page is a spoonbill.

The jackdaw of Pl. 29 is unique in decoration, and its position on the sheep's back shows good observation. The chough we have already seen in the Holkham Bible Picture Book (Pl. 10), which is probably a decade or so later; the occurrence of the species in a psalter known to have been made at Peterborough or nearby strengthens the case for the presence of the chough in the eastern counties during the Middle Ages, and so for an East Anglian origin of the Picture Book. The spoonbill also is the only complete representation of the species. While most of the birds on Pl. 29 are fairly well drawn, those in the margin of Pl. 30 are in highly unnatural attitudes, and are unlikely to have been drawn by the same man. Sandler has ascribed f. 14 to the designer-in-chief, whom she calls Master A, and the borders of f. 26 to an assistant, Master B. Is it possible that he was the artist of the Grey-Fitzpayn Hours, who had moved from the Midlands to Peterborough, and that he provided the model for part of f. 14 as well? There are further similarities between the two manuscripts.

Dñs illuminatio mea · 7 salus mea quem timebo.
Dominus ptector uite mee · a quo trepidabo.
Dum appropiant super me nocentes · ut edant carnes meas.
Qui tribulant me inimici mei · ipi infirmati sunt 7 ceciderunt.
Si consistant adusum me castra · non timebit cor meum.
Si exurgat adusum me pliuʒ · in hoc ego spabo.
Unam petii a dño hanc requiram · ut inhabitē in domo dñi omnibus diebʒ uite mee.
Ut uideam uoluntatē domini · et uisitem templum eius

Qñ abscondit me in tabernaculo suo in die malorum · ptexit me in abscondito tabernaculi sui.
In petra exaltauit me · 7 nūc exaltauit caput meū sup inimicos meos.
Circuiui 7 immolaui i tabernaculo eius hostiā uociferationis · cantabo 7 psalmum dicam dño.
Exaudi dñe uocem meā qua clamaui ad te · miserere mei 7 exaudi me.
Tibi dixit cor meū exquisiuit te facies mea · faciē tuam dñe requiram.
Ne auertas faciem tuā a me · ne declines in ira a seruo tuo.
Adiutor meus esto ne derelinquas me · neqʒ despicias me deus salutaris meus.
Qñ pater meus 7 mater mea dereliquerunt me · dñs autē assumpsit me.
Legem pone michi dñe in uia tua · et dirige me in semita recta propter inimicos meos

PLATE 31

Book of Hours. Trinity College Cambridge MS. B.11.22, f. 19r.
Probably Flemish or North French, early 14th century.

This manuscript, a contrast to the last few, was said by James (1900) to be 'almost certainly of Flemish execution' because of its resemblance to the Verdun Breviary (B.L. MS. Yates Thompson 8, and Verdun, Bibliothèque Municipale, MS. 107) and the Metz Pontifical (Fitzwilliam Museum MS. 298), which were illuminated in what is now north-east France in about 1310. All three certainly resemble each other in their drolleries — apes playing musical instruments and so on — but, seeing the Trinity manuscript three hours after examining the Pontifical, and having seen the London portion of the Breviary a week before, I noticed many differences in detail, which suggests that, if they were from the same school or workshop, they were done by different teams.

The Plate shows a hawk (with barred breast), a fair goldfinch and an excellent kingfisher, in which the only point missing is the white throat. On other pages are a good great tit (f. 200r) and parrot (f. 132v), fair chaffinches and blue tits, and a recognisable bullfinch, jay, magpie, house sparrow, wren, white stork and swan, with a few other doubtful species, including both horned and hornless owls. In the Metz Pontifical and Yates Thompson 8 the only identifiable birds are goldfinches, hawks and owls and a few domesticated species (cranes, cocks, ducks), with the addition in Yates Thompson of three magpies, and in the Metz Pontifical an all-black bird with a fox, evidently an illustration of Aesop's fable of the fox, the crow and the cheese. All the goldfinches in both manuscripts are poor; some have long tails, and some could scarcely be recognised except by comparison with the others.

While one of the artists employed on the Trinity manuscript could evidently draw birds quite well, the others in the workshop apparently could not. At this time, as at others, there was much trade between East Anglia and the Low Countries, and the architecture of King's Lynn, for example, shows much Flemish influence. Probably in manuscript illumination the current flowed in the opposite direction. Those who commissioned these books were content with much shoddier drawing than their contemporaries in England, perhaps because they were less interested in ornithology.

antate dño canticū nouū:
laus eius in ecclesia sanctorū.
etetur isrł in eo qui fecit eum: ↄ filie
syon exultent in rege suo.
audent nomen eius in choro ĩ tym-
pano et psalterio psallant ei
uia beneplacitum est domino in po-
pulo suo: et exaltauit mansuetos in

ligandos reges eorum in compe-

PLATE 32

The Grey-FitzPayn Hours. Fitzwilliam Museum MS. 242, f. 29r. English, c. 1300.

Little is known about this manuscript. The heraldry suggests that it was made for the wedding of Sir Richard Grey of Derbyshire with Joan FitzPayn, and so it can be dated to about 1300, which makes it one of the earlier Books of Hours. It has been assigned to a Midland scriptorium, is said to have East Anglian characteristics, and to show French influence. Its birds are few, but include a passable blue tit on f. 45r, and another, not so good, on f. 3r. The three birds on the plate are something of a puzzle. Hutchinson (1974) thought they were 'variations on a goldfinch', and when I first saw them in 1972 I thought that this might be true, at least of the upper one. Now that I have seen many more medieval goldfinches, including degenerate ones, I doubt this identification. In no others that I have seen is the goldfinch pattern so lost as here. Different parts of the body are red in the three birds, and in none of them is this colour as it should be for the goldfinch, or indeed for any other species; it appears to have been applied at random for effect. (There are other examples of this sort of colouring in medieval manuscripts.) Except for the red, the middle bird has very nearly the correct colouring for a cock hawfinch, and the heavy, unusual beak is in keeping. If this were so, the other two might be hasty copies, or hen birds, though the white breast, particularly of the lower bird, is difficult to explain. The hawfinch is an uncommon bird, though not difficult to see, especially in winter.

The hunting scene at the bottom should be compared with that in the Peterborough Psalter (Pl. 29).

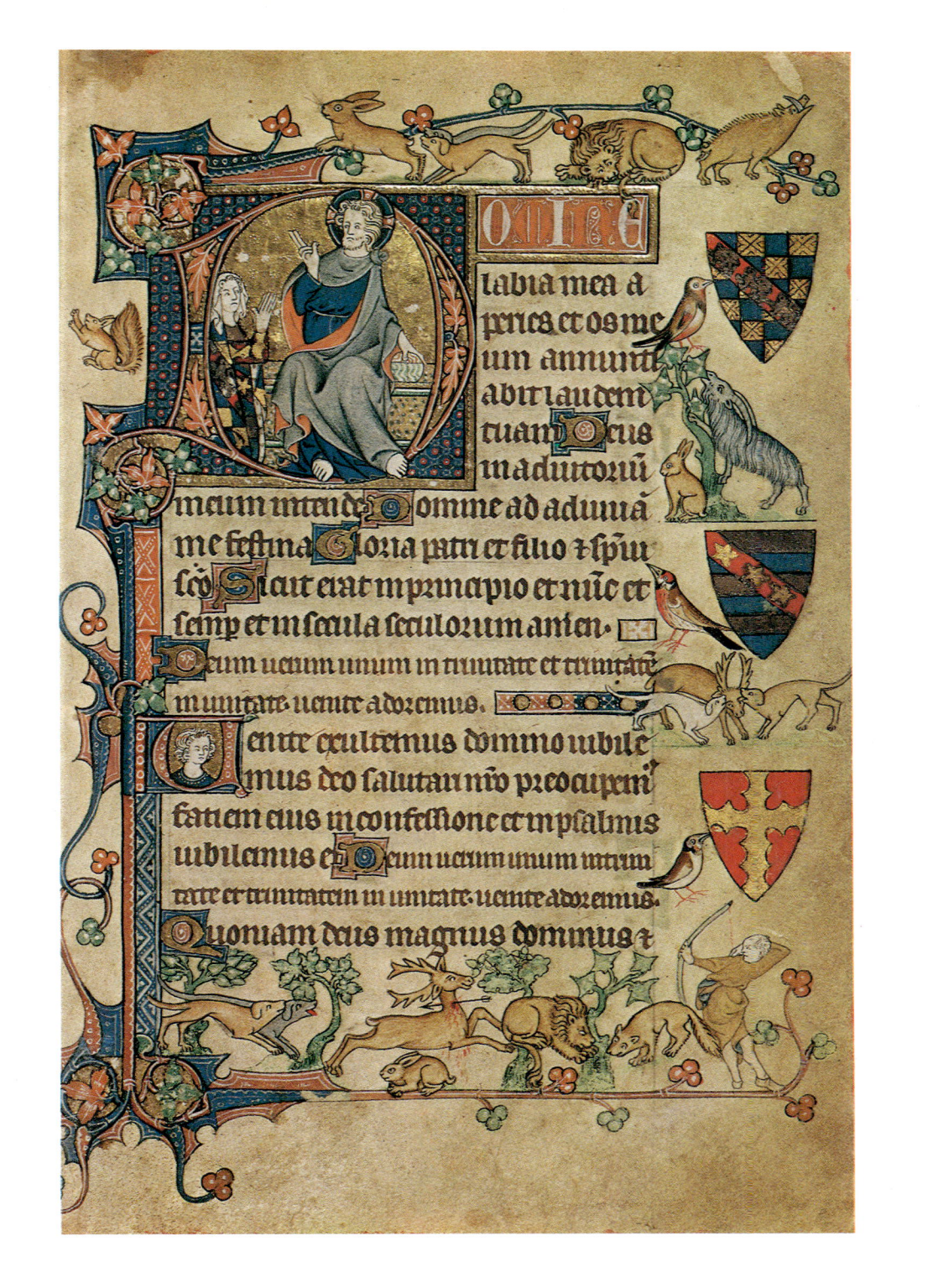

labia mea a
peries et os me
um annunti
abit laudem
tuam Deus
in adiutoriu
meum intende Domine ad adiuua
me festina Gloria patri et filio z spū
sco Sicut erat in principio et nūc et
semp et in secula seculorum amen.
Deum uerum unum in trinitate et trinitate
in unitate uenite adoremus.

Uenite exultemus dõmino iubile
mus deo salutari nõ preocupemus
faciem eius in confessione et in psalmis
iubilemus ei Deum uerum unum in trini
tate et trinitatem in unitate uenite adoremus.
Quoniam deus magnus dominus z

PLATE 33

The Bird Psalter. Fitzwilliam Museum MS. 2–1954, f. 1r. English, 1280–1300.

This Psalter includes the names of several West Country saints, and was perhaps made at Winchcombe or Gloucester; its date is about 1300 or a little earlier. It takes its name from the fact that it has drawings of about 27 species of bird, although the identity of a few of these is disputed. This is more than in any other medieval manuscript except the Sherborne Missal, and nearly twice as many as in the Alphonso Psalter. Most of them are small, but carefully drawn. Their distribution differs from that in the East Anglian psalters with birds, in that, instead of being concentrated on the pages with the few liturgical psalms, with which the daily readings of the medieval religious services began, they are scattered throughout the book. Except for Psalm 1, shown here, none of the other liturgical psalms have more than are found in many other psalms, and some have none.

The woodcock here is good, the goldfinch has too much yellow on the back; I am not sure of the identity of the bird that faces it. A robin is suggested by the thin beak, but this is a character that is often badly drawn, and neither a chaffinch nor a linnet can be ruled out.

A teal and a pied wagtail from this manuscript are shown in Pl. 48. In addition, the following species occur: crane, mallard, another duck (perhaps a smew), farmyard fowl, goose (probably domestic), gull?, owl, parrot, partridge?, stockdove?, stork?, mute swan, green woodpecker, bullfinch, jay, magpie, stonechat?, song thrush?, wren, wheatear?. There are a few others of which I can make nothing.

BEATUS UIR QUI NON AB IIT IN CONCILIO IMPIORUM

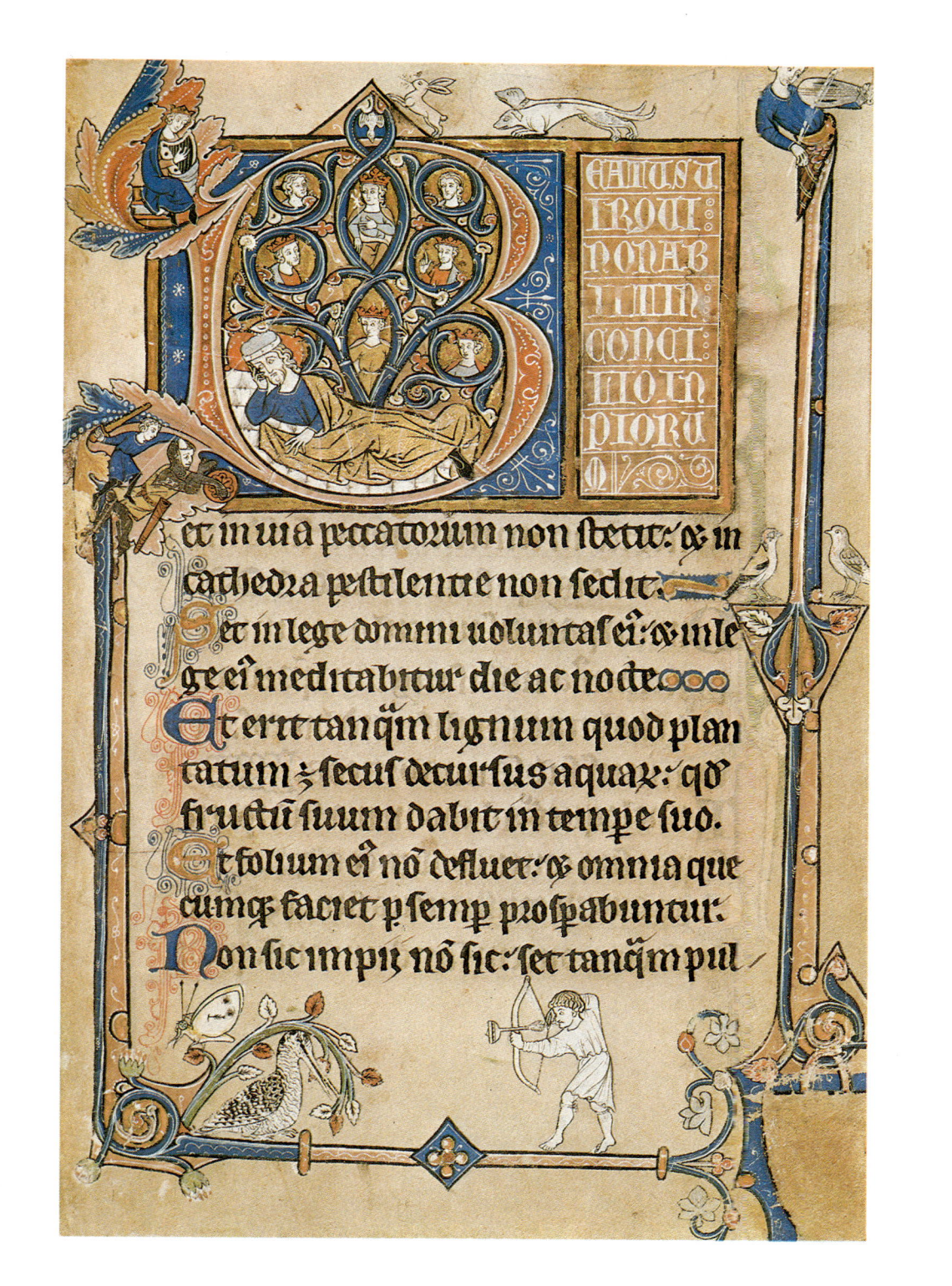

et in uia peccatorum non stetit: & in
cathedra pestilentie non sedit.
Set in lege domini uoluntas ei: & in lege ei meditabitur die ac nocte.
Et erit tanquam lignum quod plantatum ẽ secus decursus aquaru: q̇d
fructũ suum dabit in tempe suo.
Et folium ei nõ defluet: & omnia que
cumq̇ faciet p semp prospabuntur.
Non sic impii, nõ sic: set tanquam pul-

PLATE 34

The Luttrell Psalter. B.L. MS. Add. 42130. English, c. 1340. A. f. 19r; detail. B. f. 20r; detail.

The Luttrell Psalter is generally regarded as marking the culmination of the East Anglian style, and as showing signs of artistic degeneration. It is the last English manuscript to show many birds until the end of the century. Its scenes of rural life have been often used to illustrate books on the Middle Ages, but less attention has been given to the birds, of which there are 19 or 20 species, including most of those commonly illustrated. They are not, on the whole, so good as those in the Alphonso Psalter or other East Anglian manuscripts.

A. There are several scenes of geese, including two with goslings. On f. 169v the goose is white, and the five goslings brown all over, while on f. 19r, shown here, both goose and goslings are brown above and pale below, the goslings having a broad white wing-bar. This suggests that the species portrayed is either one of the wild gray geese or a domestic form showing similar features. If it is one of the former, the orange-coloured feet would suggest that the bean goose is intended, but this feature is found also in many domestic geese, and on the whole one of these is more likely. It seems that as early as the 14th century two different breeds of domesticated geese, approximating to the present-day white Embden and gray-brown Toulouse, were already in existence.

B. The starling is not common in manuscripts, the only other good one being in the Sherborne Missal. The one shown here is clearly in winter plumage, with the white-tipped feathers.

A

B

147

PLATE 35

A. Ashridge College Historia scholastica of Petrus Comestor. B.L. MS. Roy. 3 D.vi, f. 116r; detail. English, c. 1290.   B. The Smithfield Decretals. B.L. MS. Roy. 10 E.iv, f. 50r; detail. English, c. 1340.

These two close-ups have been chosen to show contrasting styles in two birds, common in the present day, that occur only rarely in English manuscripts.

The 'Historia scholastica' from which the blue tit comes is a history of the world based mainly on the Bible. This copy was made for Ashridge College, presumably between 1283 when it was founded and 1300 when the donor died. Like the Alphonso Psalter it shows Dominican influence, and was perhaps made in the same scriptorium in London or East Anglia. It has a number of birds, though not as many as the Alphonso Psalter, including a chaffinch and this blue tit which are absent from the latter. Not only is the colour of the tit very good (the white crown is missing) but the feathers of the wing-coverts, secondaries and primaries are well shown. As anyone who knows the bird can see, the jizz is very nearly perfect; probably the only recent artist who could do as well is the late Charles Tunnicliffe. The manuscript is said to show French influence; the birds show none.

The Decretals of Gregory IX from Smithfield Priory are later, about 1340, and like the Luttrell Psalter (Pl. 34) are said to be of the East Anglian school in its decline. There are more than a hundred birds, of which well over half are unrecognisable and the rest bad; the great tit shown here is the best. The head is more or less correct, but the conspicuous black breast stripe is missing, and the wing feathering and legs are shown by lines only. The manuscript is said to have been written in Italy but illustrated in England. The birds look more continental than English; cf. Pl. 46B.

A

B

PLATE 36

The Sherborne Missal. Alnwick Castle, p. 363. English, c. 1400.

The Sherborne Missal raises problems that have seldom been faced. It can be dated on internal evidence to about 1400, and was done for Sherborne Abbey in Dorset. A portrait of the chief illuminator, John Syferwas, is on p. 216; contemporary references to a Friar of that name occur from Farnham and Winchester.

The book is undoubtedly English, but it is unique for that period in being lavishly decorated with birds (and some insects) and so resembles contemporary French works. There are at least 170, of which sixty per cent are more or less certainly identifiable to 40 species. As far as p. 71 there are many imaginary birds and fantasies based on goldfinch, jay, pheasant and green woodpecker; all these look French; there are also a quite good robin, wren, crane, peacock, and pheasant, and an excellent white stork, as well as conventional doves and Johnian eagles. These last, and a very few unrecognisable birds, continue intermittently to p. 280, and in this section are six pages with some identifiable birds: pp. 188 (ostrich, quite good, but with the black and white reversed), 216 (bullfinch, goldfinch, robin?, parrot, hawk, pheasant, green woodpecker), 262 (bullfinch, goldfinch), 264 (goldfinch, magpie), 266 (a poor copy of p. 262) and 276 (peacock, pheasant). Then from pp. 363–396 is a series many of which are named in English. Finally, the last 268 pages have few birds, and these are mostly imaginary. The hand of the labelling looks contemporary with the book, but it is not that of the text; moreover it is careless scribble, many of the letters being formed in more than one way; some I find illegible, and two of the names are now meaningless. Whoever the writer was, he made mistakes: a good cock bullfinch on p. 368 is called a hen and a goldfinch on p. 384 is labelled 'A grenefỹch'. On the whole the colouring is better than the jizz, and many of the birds have been given long tails, a French feature.

Plate 36 illustrates one of the problems. The names have been read as 'mose cok' and 'mose hen', which would make the birds into titmice; however, the sexes in tits are not separable except by minute differences that are not shown here. The 'hen' might be an attempt at a blue tit; the 'cok' is no possible tit. The third letter of the names is not like the s in 'taylmose' (a fair long-tailed tit, Fig. 52) or in 'fesaunt' (p. 389). On the assumption that it might be an r and on the

(continued on p. 152)

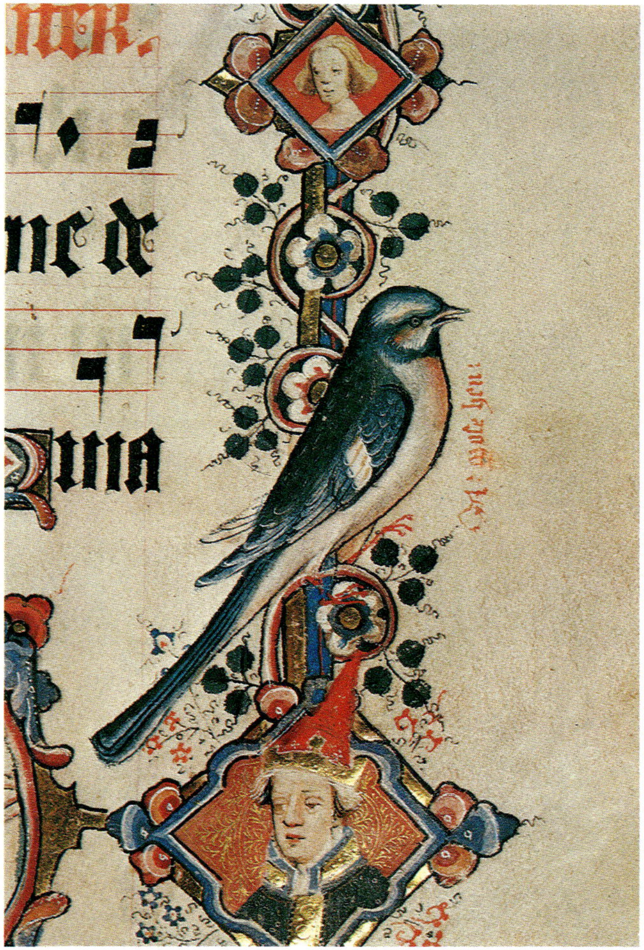

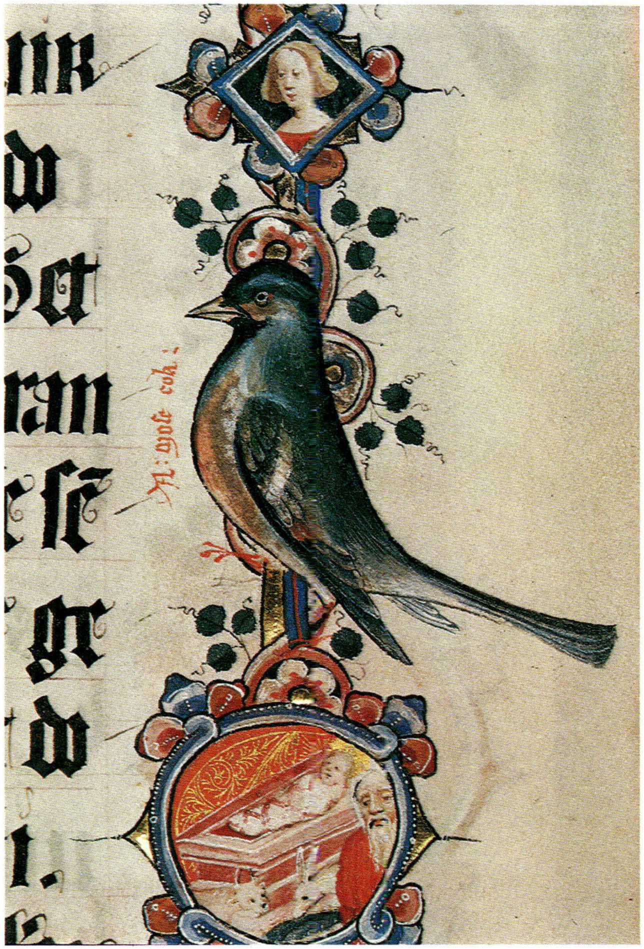

PLATE 37

The Sherborne Missal. Alnwick Castle, p. 367.

(continued from p. 150)

basis of the wedge-shaped tails I suggested in 1979 that the birds might be intended for blackcock and greyhen. Having seen the manuscript again I do not think this identification is likely, but what the birds – or the names – are I do not know.

Plate 37A shows a shrike; the flush of pink would suggest a lesser grey, which was formerly widespread in France but never, so far as is known, more than a very rare visitor to England. Superfluous pink occurs in other birds in the manuscript, and the great grey, a regular winter visitor to nothern England, is probably intended. Plate 37B is a good hen chaffinch. 'Waryghãger' is not known elsewhere, but 'weirangle' has been recorded a few times for a shrike from Shropshire northwards. The hard c in 'cayfynch' suggests a northern dialect. Many of the other birds are seabirds and some are much commoner in the north. All this suggests that the birds were drawn not by Syferwas but by a northerner who carried his sketches with him. This would help to account for the colour being better than the jizz, since the former is easier to reproduce accurately from sketches. See also Figs, 6. 18, 38, 39, 41, 52 and 53.

B

A

PLATE 38

The Lovell Lectionary. B.L. MS. Harley 7026, f. 5r. English, c. 1400.

The Lovell Lectionary, like the Sherborne Missal, is signed by John Siferwas, and much of the decoration seems to be in the same style. I do not think that the pair of birds shown here, which are the only fully natural ones in the book, can be stated with certainty to be by him. The peacock on the right is obviously carefully observed, but the other is muddled. One would expect a peahen, and the colour of the body and neck is more or less right for this; the red cheeks and wattle, the pointed tail and the absence of a crest show, however, that it is a cock pheasant. A peacock and pheasant face each other on p. 276 of the Sherborne Missal.

The only other birds are a conventional Johnian eagle, and a rather stylised but quite good crane, both on f. 11r. The Bible of Richard II (B.L. MS. Roy. 1 E.ix), sometimes associated with Siferwas, has no birds except in a Creation scene where a cock, two swans and perhaps a crane are recognisable, and the usual Tobit picture where the bird is white and not in the least like a swallow.

As far as the birds are concerned, Siferwas and his collaborators cannot be linked with any predecessors, and they reveal only a slight continental influence in the exaggerated tails of some of the birds in the Sherborne Missal, especially in the early part of the book where they were probably done by an assistant. Nor did they have any successors; in the 15th century there are hardly any English manuscripts decorated with birds. There is an early 15th-century psalter with a rather poor pheasant, jay and hawk (C.U.L. MS. Dd.12.17), but the only ones of any note are the group of which the next plate is an example and probably the type.

PLATE 39

Sir Peter Idley's Instructions. C.U.L. MS. Ee.4.37, f. 1r. English, mid-15th century.

This is one of the few non-religious English manuscripts with some decorated pages, and one of the latest to have any birds, its date being probably in the 1460s. The general effect of the page shown is very similar to that of contemporary French or Flemish works, and Scott (1968) has suggested that two artists were employed, one of whom was Franco-Flemish trained. This is supported by the fact that the owl has the general appearance and shape of head and facial disc of the little owl, a bird that was unlikely to have been present in England at that time. The peacock could have been done anywhere; the yellow and black bird at top right was possibly based on a goldfinch, but it is nearer in colour to a golden oriole. If this is the correct identification, the continental origin of the artist, if not of the manuscript, is confirmed. There is another owl on f. 27r, which is a poor copy of that on f. 1 with much less careful drawing of the feathers, and was probably done by an assistant.

Scott has grouped with this manuscript four others, on the ground that they include the same owl. They do indeed have owls of much the same shape, but some of the features that she noted as characteristic of the artist are in fact characteristic of the little owl, and an ornithologist accustomed to take note of details of plumage can see that each is unique. Those in Lambeth MS. 186, f. 109r (a Psalter) and Bodleian Library MS. Rawlinson poetry 223, f. v look like poor copies of the one in this plate. Owls on f. 1r of Lambeth MS. 186, on f. 29r of Harley MS. 2887 (a Book of Hours) (Fig. 59) and f. 1r of Bodley MS. 283 (The Mirror of the World) are probably copies, but might just possibly be original. Little owls were used on the continent as decoys by bird-catchers, so that it would have been easy for an artist to get hold of one to draw from.

The Harley and Lambeth manuscripts have also two peacocks each. The two Lambeth peacocks are alike, but they differ from the other three, each of which is unique, so that there are four types of peacock altogether, suggesting four artists.

Item mei tractatus sit in noie dni mei Jhu xpi
    ...ug io bona cuncta pcedut Et a quo est oie datu
    optimu et oie donu pfectu descendens a pre
    luminu Quarto amore quanta q dilectione
    mei paterna caritas tuam diligat filialem sub
    iectione dico tibi possem narrare lingua mea possem
    aliquatenus explicari volens igitur Ego Petrus
    Idle Armig te filium meum Thomam bonis morib
    conformare do de amore et dilectione dei et proxi
    ac aliaz reruz nection de forma honeste vite instruere

In the begynnyng of this litell werke
I pray to god my penne he lede
ffor in makyng I am as a yonge clerke
That lerneth first cristis crosse me spede
But that nature dryueth me to this dede
As y can to teche the my childe
That art yet yonge and somdele wylde

ffirst god and thy kyng yt love and drede
Abone all thyngis yt tho pserue
ffaile not this for no manes nede
Thoughe thow therfore shold pissh and sterue
A man ony tyme fro his trowthe to swerue
Hym silf and his kynne doth grete shame
Therfore eu kepe the fro suche maner blame

Allso thy fader and moder thow honowre
As y wolde thy sue shold to the
And euy man aftir riche and powre
As eu thow wilt haue loue of me
And in reward it is gode vnto the
Thy blessyngs of thy fader and moder
Gode kepe that and desire noon other

PLATE 40

Cocharelli: Tractatus de vitiis septem. B.L. MS. Egerton 3127, f. 1v. Italian, late 14th century.

The Cocharelli Treatise on the seven vices is in four sections in the British Library (Add. 27695 and 28841, Egerton 3127 and 3781), all containing pages with birds, and, even more interesting, insects and other invertebrates. It is Italian, from near Genoa, and has been ascribed to an artist named Cybo d'Hyères, who some say did not exist. Both the page shown here, and f. 1r of Add. 28841, have many birds of several species scattered all over them. At the top of the Plate is a scene of carrion-eaters. The black birds on the left are presumably ravens, since the normal crow of Italy is the grey and black hoody. The next bird is certainly a vulture and possibly a lammergeier, which is known to have nested at one time in Italy, though it does so no longer, and then there are two kites, but whether black or red is uncertain. The colour is nearer the black but the deeply forked tail suggests the red; both species breed in Italy at the present day. Other birds that can be recognised are hawks attacking perhaps a crane and a pheasant, goldfinches, magpies, an eagle with a nest and young, a covey of red-legged partridges and another probably of grey partridges, a jay, white storks and ducks. The best are perhaps the hoopoes, which show the contrasting appearance of the flat and erect crest (Fig. 44).

Pächt (1950) regarded this manuscript as the 'immediate antecedent' to the Sketchbook of Giovannino dei Grassi, which has several water colours of birds. To judge from the facsimile (Giovannino dei Grassi, 1961) they are stiff and not in the least like the birds in the Cocharelli Treatise, but they do resemble those in the contemporary Pepysian Sketchbook (Pl. 2).

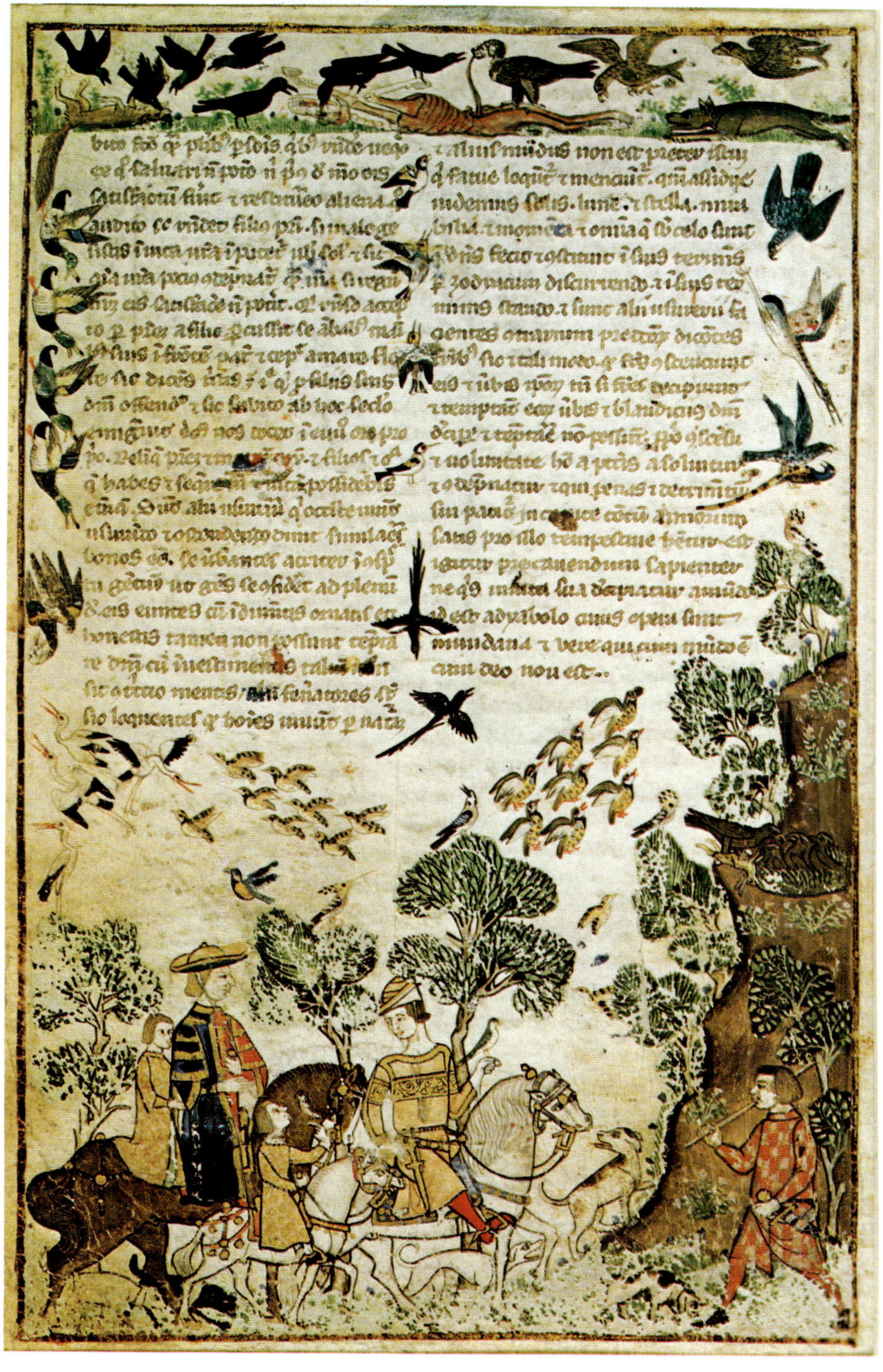

PLATE 41

Cocharelli: Tractatus de vitiis septem. B.L. MS. Add. 27695, f. 4r; detail.

At first glance I thought this bird was a gannet, and indeed the black and white pattern and the jizz fit this better than anything else. But the pouch under the beak, which until the picture is enlarged looks like a part of the background pattern, shows that it is a pelican. It is clearly derived from a real bird, but looks as if it were copied from a better drawing; the pouch is too square at the corners. There are two species of pelican in the Mediterranean, the Dalmatian and the white, and although neither now breeds in Italy there has been much reduction in recent years and both could have been common there in the 14th century. Of the two, the white pelican seems the more likely.

The birds at the bottom, though too blue, must be great tits, out of scale and out of place. Two more, distorted, pelicans fill the corresponding corners above.

Pelicanus of the bestiaries is a bird that pecks its breast and so produces a stream of blood that revives and nourishes its young. It thus becomes a symbol of the Resurrection. Its representation is found not only in bestiaries, but in many other manuscripts and in sculpture, especially in misericords. It can be seen in the Holkham Bible Picture Book (Plate 11A) where it looks like a sparrowhawk, and in the Flemish Bartholomew (Pl. 19) where it is too small to be recognisable. The only other representations of real pelicans that I know are in the *De arte venandi cum avibus*, where there are several. It is not surprising that French and English artists did not know it.

161

PLATE 42

Hours of Jeanne de Navarre. B.N. Nouv.aq.lat.3145, f. 55v. French, c. 1340.

With this Book of Hours by the Parisian miniaturist Jean Le Noir, which is contemporary with the Luttrell Psalter (Pl. 34), we come to the beginning of the characteristically French use of birds, which culminates in the 15th century. The goldfinch at the top and the robin-like bird at the bottom might have been done by an East Anglian artist. On the top left is what is fairly obviously a spotted woodpecker (though Avril (1978) or his translator calls it a green woodpecker). The barred wings, short tail and absence of red from the head suggest a female lesser spotted. But that species is elusive, and seldom seen close to, so that it seems unlikely. The colour pattern is in any case not quite correct and a female great spotted may be intended. The bird below, presumably a swallow, is in a totally different style. This impressionistic type of drawing, with fuzzy edges and lack of detail, is characteristically French, and continues for more than a century. It leads to the portrayal of birds in unnatural attitudes, and to purely imaginary species (cf. Pl. 19).

cede. p dnm nrm ihm xpm filium tuu. qui te
cum uiuit et regnat in unitate spiritus sancti
deus p omnia secula seculor. Amen. Do
mine exaudi orationem meam. Et clamor
meus ad te ueniat. Benedicamus domino.
Deo gracias. Anime omnium fidelium defunc
torum p misericordiam dei requiescant i pace. am.

PLATE 43

Missal of St. Denys. Victoria and Albert Musuem MS. 1346–1891, f. 284v. French, c. 1350.

According to Avril (1978), the illuminator of this manuscript, whom he calls 'the artist of Le Remède de Fortune', from a manuscript in the Bibliothèque National (Fr. 1586), was 'the true creator of that naturalism which began to triumph in French illumination under the reign of Charles V' [1380–1422]. However true that may be of the scenes in the little pictures in the text, it is far from true of the birds in the borders, as anyone who knows them can see; they may well have been done by an assistant. This page shows some of the best. The great tit at the top is reasonably correct in colouring, but the feet are unnatural and the upward bent tail is impossible. The wren on the left is perhaps a little better, but the most one can say for the bird at the base is that it is presumably intended to be a swallow. In addition to another wren, another swallow and several great tits of varying degress of inaccuracy, there are on other pages a few goldfinches, three possible blue tits and a possible hoopoe, three parrots, and conventional owls, stork-like birds, ducks, a dove and a vulture. Of all these the only ones that I did not, in going through the book, annotate in some derogatory way, were four great tits. Sixty-seven I marked as 'poor', and 51 as 'unrecognisable' out of a total of 126, so that we are halfway to the final ornithological degeneration which, as I have said in the Introduction, is reached in some Flemish manuscripts of the end of the 15th century. (For illustrations, see Alexander, 1970.)

at sue michele festimtati. Ofini
Epl̄ Ab inicio et an secl̄a. xvj.
xvj. R. Propter veritate. xvj. v.
Si est dn̄ia. Alla. d. Virū electa.
xvj. vij. Sequēcia. Hac clara die
Euāgl̄ Extollēges maria. vij.
No dicatur Credo. ū sic dc̄. Offe.
Offeretur. hympni. xvj. vij. Secr.
Magna ē dn̄e apud cleme
ciam tuā dī genitric orō
quam idco de plēn sec̄lo subtra
histi. ut p ptīs nr̄is apud te fiduci
aat ītercedat. per eūd. presac.
Et te ī assūpcōne. com.
Diffusa est gracia. xvj. vij. postc̄.
Concede misericors deus
fragilitati nr̄e psidiū
ut q̄ sc̄e dei genitricis requiē cele
bramus ītercessiōis ei auxilio
a nr̄is iniquitatibus relē
uemur per. In die officiū.

cele brantes sub honore
marie virginis de cuius as
sumpcione gaudent an
ge li et collaudant filiū
meum. Seculorum amē. oid.
Concēdā nob dn̄e
huius diei festiu
itas ope obseat sa
lutaris i qua sc̄a dei genitrix
mortem subijt temporalē. nec
tam mortis nexibz deprimi
potuit. q̄ eiundem filiū tuū dn̄m
nr̄m de se genuit incarnatū.
Qui teciū. lc̄o lib̄i sapiēcie
Ab ōibz regē ēsiui. et ī
hereditate dn̄i morabor.
Tūc precepit et dī michi
creator ōiū. et q̄ creauit
me requieuit ī tabernaclo mo
ee dicit michi In iacob inha

Laudamus omnis in domino diem festum

PLATE 44

Hours of Etienne Chevalier. B.L. MS. Add. 16997, f. 21r. French, early 15th century.

Meiss (1968), basing himself on style and not on documentary evidence, says that the illustrations in this book were planned, and to a large extent executed, by the anonymous artist known as 'the Boucicaut Master'. With that I am in no position to disagree, but he goes on to say that the border of f. 21r, shown here, is 'by a crude assistant'. So far as the birds are concerned, this is the opposite of the truth, since they are much better than most of the others in the book and than the generality of 15th-century French birds, such as those in the Books of Hours of John Duke of Berry. In particular the two owls (top right and middle left) are good representations of long-eared owls (Fig. 23). This is interesting, because although owls are one of the commonest of all birds occurring in manuscripts, they are nearly always conventional (Figs. 19–22). The tawny in the Ormesby Psalter (Pl. 24), the little owl in Sir Peter Idley's Instructions (Pl. 39), and some (notably a barn owl on f. 10r) in the *De arte venandi cum avibus*, are the only others known to me that are well drawn from life. The long-eared owls here should be compared with those in the next plate.

Other birds here are: half way down on the right-hand border, a rather poor peacock, with no crest and a tail that is difficult to see and hardly connected to the body, and a probable turtle dove; at the bottom, a fair hen pheasant and a goldfinch; and at the top of the left-hand border a bird which, to judge from its cocked-up tail, is presumably intended for a wren, though it is not much like one.

Domine labia mea aperies. Et os meum annunciabit laudem tuam.

PLATE 45

Hours of Etienne Chevalier. B.L. MS. Add. 16997, f. 145r.

This page is a contrast to the last. The two owls at the bottom have reverted toward the usual convention, and are unlikely to have been done by the same man as the long-eareds of f. 21r. The goldfinch at the top left is without some of his colours, and has the characteristically French fuzzy outline. On the right the hen chaffinch is also fuzzy, though the drawing is better. This fuzziness is found also, if the reproductions that I have seen are to be trusted, in the birds of four Books of Hours of the Duke of Berry, which are contemporary with those of Etienne Chevalier, or a little earlier.

omine labia me
a aperies.
Et os meum
annuntiabit laudem tuam.

PLATE 46

Hours of Etienne Chevalier. B.L. MS. Add. 16997.   A. f. 138v; detail.   B. f. 163r; detail.

These two drawings illustrate on the one hand the quality sometimes reached by French artists in their drawings of birds, and on the other their much more usual manner, which is almost baroque, or even rococo.

A. The bird, whatever the species, has excellent jizz for a finch, and the beak is well drawn. A bird-watcher failing to see much detail would probably call it 'a little brown job'; it is most likely a hen linnet. We know that linnets were among the birds kept in the royal aviaries in the 15th century, and at that time noblemen and rich commoners also kept captive birds. Many of the birds mentioned in the royal accounts, such as various finches, parrots, pheasants and turtle-doves, are illustrated in Books of Hours.

B. The bird is obviously a great tit, a species common in French manuscripts, rare in English, not mentioned as being kept in captivity. The bird here is fuzzy, in an unnatural attitude, (note the right wing) and entirely French. Although the fuzziness of the edges is exaggerated by the magnification, it is visible in the manuscript in both these birds.

Other birds in the Hours of Etienne Chevalier are: crane, duck of indeterminate species, a sparrowhawk or goshawk, robin, green woodpecker and hoopoe.

There is another and better known Book of Hours of Etienne Chevalier, who was royal treasurer to Charles VII, at Chantilly.

A

B

171

PLATE 47

The London Hours of René of Anjou. B.L. MS. Egerton 1070, f. 34v. French, c. 1410.

These Hours are ten or twenty years earlier than those of Etienne Chevalier. The artist responsible for them is called 'The Egerton Master', but Meiss (1968) thinks that his workshop collaborated with that of the Boucicaut Master on this book. The plate should therefore be compared with Pls. 44 and 45.

If the tail is diagnostic, the bird at top left is a wren; except in general shape it is not much like that in Pl. 44. Next to it is a peacock, much better drawn than the one in Etienne Chevalier. At bottom right is a cock chaffinch, again much better than the chaffinch in Pl. 45. On the left is a pale green parrot (too yellow in the manuscript), which has a good collar and the usual divided tail; Etienne Chevalier has no parrots. Above the parrot is a bird that is probably intended for a green woodpecker, though if it is there are several errors; notably, the tail is too short and there is a pink flush on the breast. The same bird occurs on five other pages; there is one green woodpecker in Etienne Chevalier (f. 146v), which is much more like the real thing and quite different from those of René of Anjou. Altogether the birds do not suggest any collaboration.

According to Loisel (1912) René of Anjou possessed at Angers the biggest menagerie of the 15th century, so that the birds in his Hours are surprisingly few. Other birds besides those shown are a Johnian eagle, hoopoe, pheasant, owl, goldfinch and what is probably a robin.

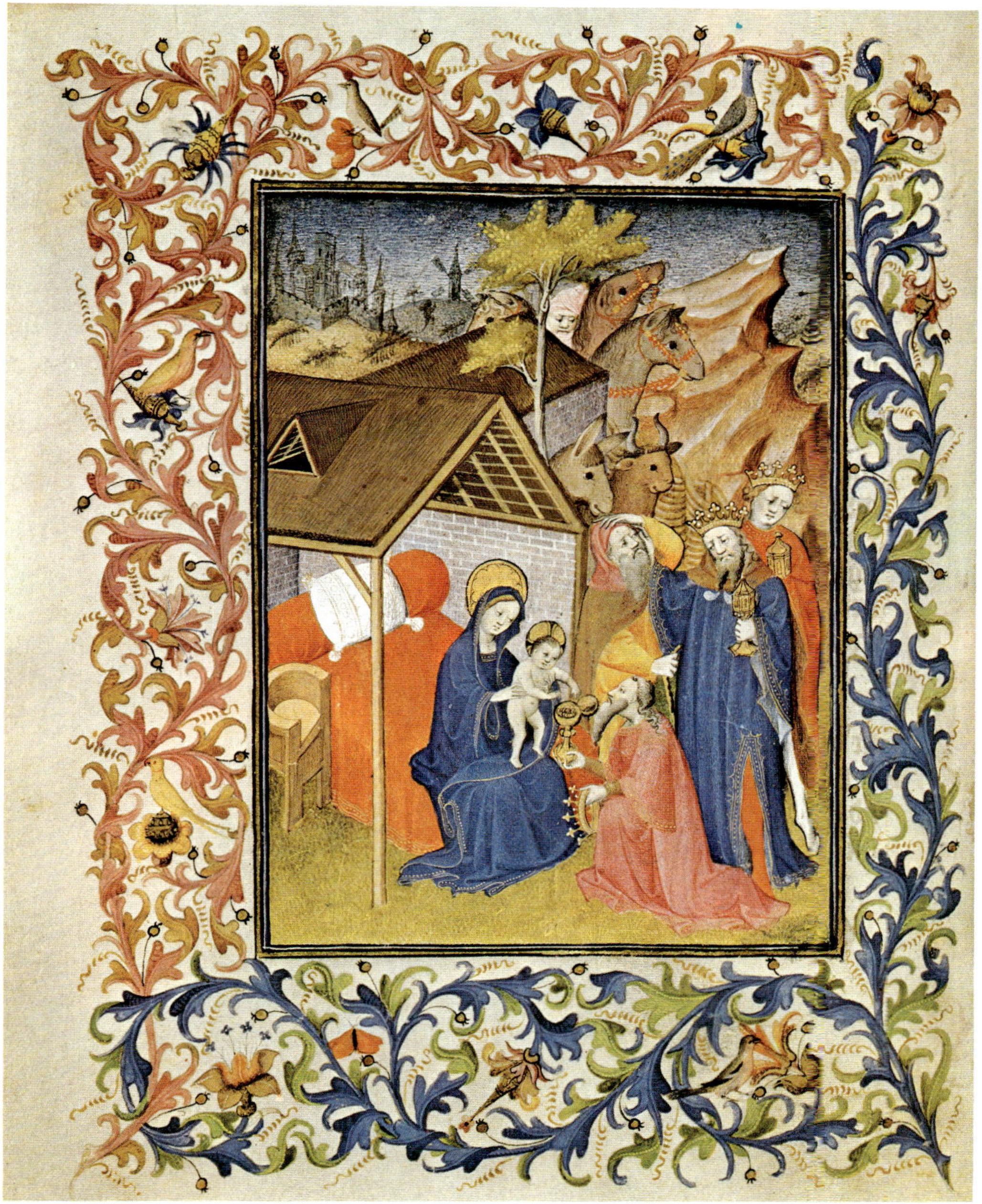

PLATE 48

A. The Bird Psalter. Fitzwilliam Museum MS. 2–1954, f. 74v.
B. The Bird Psalter. Fitzwilliam Museum MS. 2–1954, f. 3r.
C. Digestum. Hereford Cathedral MS. P.7.v., f. 12r. English, 13th century.
D. Gregorii Moralia. Emmanuel College Cambridge MS. 112, f. 180v.
English, early 14th century.

A. This is an excellent drake teal. There are plenty of white domestic ducks and of the common wild mallard, especially the more colourful drakes, in manuscripts, but the only other teals are a drake and a duck, both labelled 'Tel' in the Sherborne Missal, where the jizz is not so good as here.

B. The bird shown here, and another on f. 84v, are the only good wagtails in English manuscripts except for one in the Sherborne Missal.

C. This manuscript is dated by the script to the 13th century, and is presumably late. It has only a few other birds, of which only one other thrush, and this one, which is the best song thrush that I have seen, are identifiable.

D. This copy of the works of Gregory the Great has been ascribed to the East Anglian school, and its decorations are said to be by the artist who illuminated ff. 55v and 147v (among others) of the Ormesby Psalter (Pls. 25, 26), but the few birds that it contains give no support to this view. The bird shown here has a moustachial stripe, and so may be intended to be a peregrine, in spite of the barred breast; if so, it is one of the very few falcons, as distinct from hawks, in English medieval art.

A B C D

THE REFERENCES: a note for the reader

In large libraries, each manuscript is known by a number; it may be a shelf-number or press-mark, an accession number or a running number in a standard catalogue. Many important manuscripts have also what may be called a pet-name, by which they are commonly known to scholars. When this is unique, e.g. The Alphonso Psalter, I have generally used this. I have avoided ambiguous names such as the Arundel Psalter, often used for B.L. MS. Arundel 83, since there are other psalters in that collection. The number is given at least on first mention, either in the caption of a figure or plate, or in the text.

Some libraries, for example the British Library and the Bodleian Library, number their various special collections of manuscripts separately. In such cases, where the name of the collection, e.g. the Harley MSS, is unambiguous, I have not always repeated the name of the Library. The following abbreviations are used in this connexion:

- B.L. British Library Reference Division (formerly the British Museum (B.M.) Library)
- B.N. Bibliothèque Nationale, Paris
- C.U.L. Cambridge University Library.

Manuscripts are usually foliated, i.e. numbered by leaves or folios (abbreviated f. or ff.), rather than paginated, i.e. numbered by page (p. or pp.), as is the case with printed books, but there are exceptions such as the Sherborne Missal, which is paginated. Each folio has two sides, known as the recto (abbreviated r) and verso (v). An open manuscript therefore presents to the reader the verso of one folio on the left and, on the right, the recto of the next.

The black-and-white illustrations in the Introduction are referred to as Figures (Fig.) and the colour illustrations as Plates (Pl.).

References to printed works are given according to the Harvard system, under which only the surname of the author and the date of publication of the work in question are given in the main text, the key being provided by the Bibliography which is arranged alphabetically by author.

BIBLIOGRAPHY

This bibliography includes only books and papers that are especially relevant to the theme of the book. There are many others that deal with the manuscripts mentioned, either in general or in particular, but, so far as I am aware, only those listed here are worth looking at in connexion with the birds. I have not given references for general statements about the provenance or date of manuscripts on which there seems to be general agreement, but they can mostly be traced in Rickert (1965) and Robb (1973), which, together with the published catalogues of several libraries, have been my chief guides. Similarly, statements about birds, where they do not come from my own experience, have mostly been checked from Cramp and Simmons (1977–; only two volumes have yet been published), Voous (1960), and Witherby (1944). The place of publication is London unless it is stated otherwise.

Alexander, J. J. G.
1970: *The Master of Mary of Burgundy: a Book of Hours for Engelbert of Nassau.*

1978: *The decorated letter.*

Avril, F.
1978: *Manuscript painting at the Court of France: the fourteenth century (1310–1380).*

Backhouse, J. M.
1979: *The illuminated manuscript.*

Brieger, P. H. (ed.)
1967: *Facsimile of the Apocalypse Trinity College Cambridge R.16.2.*, 2 Vols.

Brown, G. Baldwin
1921: *The arts in early England,* Vol. 5.

Cecchelli, C., Furlani, G., and Salmi, M.
1959: *The Rabula Gospels,* Olten.

Cramp, S., and Simmons, K. E. L. (eds.)
1977–: *The Birds of the Western Palearctic,* Oxford.

Dodwell, C. R.
1959: *The great Lambeth Bible.*

Evans, A. H. (ed.)
1903: *Turner on Birds,* Cambridge.

Frederick II
1969: *De arte venandi cum avibus,* Facsimile, with Commentary by C. A. Willemsen, Graz; Codices e Vaticani Selecti XXX. 2 vols.

Giovannino de Grassi
1961: *Taccuino di disegni,* Facsimile, with anonymous introduction, Bergamo (Monumenta Bergomensia V).

Harthan, J.
1977: *Books of Hours and their owners.*

Hassall, W. O.
1954: *The Holkham Bible Picture Book.*

Henry, F.
1974: *The Book of Kells.*

Howe, W. N.
1912: *Animal life in Italian painting.*

Hutchinson, G. E.
1974: 'Attitudes towards nature in medieval England: The Alphonso and Bird Psalters', *Isis,* Vol. 65, pp. 5–37.

1978: 'Zoological iconography in the West after A.D.1200', *American Scientist,* Nov.–Dec. 1978, pp. 675–84.

Ives, S. A., and Lehmann-Haupt, H.
1942: *An English thirteenth century bestiary: a new discovery in the technique of medieval illumination,* New York.

James, M. R.
1900: *The western manuscripts in the library of Trinity College Cambridge,* Vol. 1, Cambridge.

1909: *A reproduction in facsimile of the Trinity College Apocalypse, MS.R.16.2.*

1925: 'An English medieval sketchbook, No. 1916 in the Pepysian Library, Magdalene College Cambridge', *Walpole Society,* Vol. 13, pp. 1–17.

1927: *The Apocalypse in Latin: MS.10 in the collection of Dyson Perrins, F.S.A.,* Oxford.

1928: *The Bestiary ... MS.Ii.4.26 ... in the University Library, Cambridge,* Oxford.

1931: *The Apocalypse in art: Schweich Lectures of the British Academy 1927.*

1932: *A descriptive catalogue of the manuscripts in the library of Lambeth Palace: the medieval manuscripts,* Cambridge.

Kendrick, T. D., Brown, T. J., Bruce-Mitford, R. L. S., Roosen-Runge, H., Ross, A. S. C., Stanley, E. G., and Werner, A. E. A.
1960: *Evangeliorum quattuor Codex Lin-*

disfarnensis, Vol. 2, Olten & Lausanne.

Klingender, F. (ed. E. Antal and J. Harthan)
1971: *Animals in art and thought to the end of the Middle Ages.*

Loisel, G.
1912: *Histoire des ménageries,* Paris, 3 vols.

Longnon, J., and Cazelles, R. (eds.)
1969: *Les très riches Heures du Duc de Berry.*

McCulloch, F.
1962: *Medieval Latin and French bestiaries,* 2nd ed., Chapel Hill, North Carolina (Studies in the Romance Languages and Literatures 33).

Martindale, A.
1967: *Gothic Art.*

Meiss, M.
1968: *French painting in the time of Jean de Berry: the Boucicault Master.*

Pächt, O.
1943: 'A Giottesque episode in English medieval art', *Journal of the Warburg and Courtauld Institutes,* Vol. 6, pp. 51–70.

1950: 'Early Italian nature studies and the early calendar landscape', *Journal of the Warburg and Courtauld Institutes,* Vol. 13, pp. 13–47.

Ray, J.
1678: *The ornithology of Francis Willughby.* Facsimile reprint, Chichely 1972.

Rickert, M.
1965: *Painting in Britain: the Middle Ages,* 2nd ed., Harmondsworth (The Pelican History of Art).

Robb, D. M.
1973: *The art of the illuminated manuscript.* South Brunswick and New York, London, Yoseloff.

Sandler, L. F.
1974: *The Peterborough Psalter in Brussels and other Fenland manuscripts.*

Scheller, R. W.
1963: *A survey of medieval model books.*

Scott, K. A.
1968: 'A mid-fifteenth century illuminating shop and its customers', *Journal of the Warburg and Courtauld Institutes,* Vol. 31, pp. 170–96.

Sweet, H.
1885: *The oldest English texts,* Early English Text Society, Vol. 83.

Thomas, M.
1979: *The Golden Age: manuscript painting in the time of Jean, Duc de Berry.*

Ticehurst, N. F.
1957: *The mute swan in England.*

Tristram, H. B.
1873: *The natural history of the Bible*, 3rd ed.

Vaurie, C.
1971: 'Birds in the prayer-book of Bonne of Luxembourg', *Bulletin of the Metropolitan Museum of Art New York,* Vol. 29, pp. 279–81.

Voous, K. H.
1960: *Atlas of European birds.*

Webster, J. C.
1938: *The Labours of the months,* Princeton, New Jersey.

White, T. H.
1954: *The book of beasts, being a translation from the Latin bestiary.*

Witherby, H. F. (ed.)
1944: *The handbook of British birds.*

Wright, T.
1884: *Anglo-Saxon and Old English vocabularies,* 2nd ed., rev. R. P. Wülcker.

Yapp, W. B.
1979: 'The birds of English medieval manuscripts', *Journal of medieval history,* Vol. 5, pp. 315–48.

1981: 'Birds in captivity in the Middle Ages', *Archives of Natural History,* Vol. 10.

ACKNOWLEDGEMENTS

The British Library Board and the author would like to acknowledge with gratitude the co-operation of all those who provided photographs of manuscripts in their collections for inclusion in this book, namely:

Bibliothèque Nationale, Paris (Pl. 42), Bibliothèque Royale Albert Ier, Brussels (Pls. 29,30), Bodleian Library, Oxford (Pls. 12B, 17B, 24–26; Figs. 26, 30, 57), British Museum (Fig. 60), Cambridge University Library (Pls. 14, 39; Fig. 49), Emmanuel College, Cambridge (Pl. 48D), Fitzwilliam Museum, Cambridge (Pls. 32, 33, 48A,B; Fig. 5), Hereford Cathedral Chapter Library (Pl. 48C), John Rylands University Library, Manchester (Fig. 58), Lambeth Palace Library (Fig. 54), Lincoln College, Oxford (Fig. 40), Magdalene College (Pepysian Library), Cambridge (Pl. 2; Figs. 16, 42, 45), New College, Oxford (Pl. 16), H.G. The Duke of Northumberland (Pls. 32, 33; Figs. 6, 18, 38, 39, 41, 52, 53), Österreichische Nationalbibliothek, Vienna (Fig. 46), Sidney Sussex College, Cambridge (Pl. 12A; Figs. 7, 29), Trinity College, Cambridge (Pls. 13, 31; Figs. 9, 31, 42, 45, 48), Trinity College, Dublin (Pl. 5; Figs. 13, 14). Victoria & Albert Museum (Pl. 43).

The photographs of the Sherborne Missal and of the British Library's own manuscripts were taken by members of the British Library Photographic Service. Mrs Sally Brown, Miss Janet Backhouse and Mrs Ann Payne, all of the Department of Manuscripts, provided special assistance in the preparation of this book.

INDEXES Numbers in **bold** are those of the colour plates, and in *italic* are those of the black and white figures. Numbers in roman refer to pages. Mentions of a bird or manuscript on the page facing a plate where it is illustrated, or on the same page as a figure, are not separately entered.

INDEX OF BIRDS

A. English and other vernacular names.

Auer-caillie 31
Auerhoen, Auerhuhn 31

Bee-eater *Merops apiaster* Linnaeus 53
Bergandir 31
Bittern *Botaurus stellaris* (Linnaeus) 18
Blackbird *Turdus merula* Linnaeus **2, 21, 29;** *51;* 64, 65, 98, 118
Blackcap *Sylvia atricapilla* (Linnaeus) 70
Blackcock *Lyrurus tetrix* (Linnaeus) 152
Bornet 32
Bullfinch *Pyrrhula pyrrhula* (Linnaeus) **1, 10, 11A, 15, 27;** *21, 40;* 52, 58, 59, 116, 140, 144, 150
Buntings Emberizidae 60
Bunting, black-headed *Emberiza melanocephala* Scopoli 60, 82
Bustards Otididae 92
Buzzard *Buteo buteo* (Linnaeus) 33

Capercaillie *Tetrao urogallus* Linnaeus **23,** *17;* 31, 120
Ceo 57
Chaffinch *Fringilla coelebs* Linnaeus **33, 37B, 45, 47;** 58, 59, 60, 64, 75, 78, 140, 144, 148
Chough *Pyrrhocorax pyrrhocorax* (Linnaeus) **10, 29;** 56, 57, 138
Cock see fowl
Coot *Fulica atra* Linnaeus 11, 49
Cormorant *Phalacrocorax carbo* (Linnaeus) *39;* 47, 49, 86

Crane *Grus grus* (Linnaeus) **1, 7, 8, 10, 13A, 14, 15, 19, 21, 28, 29, 40;** *2, 3, 11, 40;* 12, 13–16, 18, 75, 90, 92, 96, 102, 118, 140, 144, 150, 154, 170
Crossbill *Loxia curvirostra* Linnaeus *46;* 59, 60
Crow **16;** 30, 56–57, 94, 110, 124, 140
Crow, carrion *Corvus corone corone* Linnaeus **19;** 56
Crow, hoody *Corvus corone cornix* Linnaeus **19;** 56, 158
Cuckoo *Cuculus canorus* Linnaeus 53
Curlew *Numenius arquata* (Linnaeus) *42;* 52

Dipper *Cinclus cinclus* (Linnaeus) 68, 118
Dove *Columba livia* Gmelin **9, 14;** *34, 35, 36;* 13, 26, 44–46, 53, 84, 94, 128, 150, 164
Dove, stock *Columba oenas* Linnaeus **28;** *2;* 46, 144
Dove, turtle *Streptopelia turtur* (Linnaeus) **44;** 46, 78, 170
Duck **2, 10, 28, 40;** *2, 3, 11, 60;* 13, 16, 23–24, 31, 90, 92, 122, 140, 144, 164, 170, 174
Duck, wild see Mallard
Eagle **3, 8, 14, 18, 40;** *13, 14;* 13, 19, 26–27, 33, 45, 92, 96, 150, 154, 172
Eagle, golden *Aquila chrysaetos* (Linnaeus) 84
Eagle, white-tailed *Haliaetus albicilla* (Linnaeus) 114

Falcon 33–34

Falcon, peregrine *Falco peregrinus* Tunstal **48D;** 33, 122, 174
Fieldfare *Turdus pilaris* Linnaeus 53, 64
Finches Fringillidae 58–60, 170
Fowl, farmyard *Gallus* sp. **6, 8, 9, 19, 29;** 19–20, 35, 92, 96, 140, 144, 154
Fowl, guinea *Numida meleagris* Linnaeus 31, 92
Fugeldoppe 49

Gannet *Sula bassana* (Linnaeus) *38;* 47, 160
Goldfinch *Carduelis carduelis* (Linnaeus) **1, 10, 11A, 11B, 15, 24, 27, 28, 29, 31, 33, 40, 42, 44, 45;** *2, 21, 56;* 12, 52, 58, 59, 75, 76, 78, 116, 140, 142, 150, 154, 164, 172
Goose **14, 34A;** 23, 24, 96, 108, 144
Goose, barnacle *Branta leucopsis* (Bechstein) *18;* 32, 49
Goose, bean *Anser fabalis* (Latham) 146
Goose, grey lag *Anser anser* (Linnaeus) 23, 31–32
Goshawk *Accipiter gentilis* (Linnaeus) **22, 24, 29;** 33, 34, 170
Greenfinch *Carduelis chloris* (Linnaeus) **26;** 59
Grouse, black *Lyrurus tetrix* (Linnaeus) 31, 152
Grouse, red *Lagopus lagopus* (Linnaeus) 31
Gull 76 144
Gull, common *Larus canus* Linnaeus **1;** *37;* 47

183

Gull, herring *Larus argentatus*
   Pontopidan   **16;** 12, 47, 49, 82

Hawfinch *Coccothraustes coccothraustes* (Linnaeus)   **26, 30, 32;** 59, 78
Hawk   **8, 14, 16, 28, 31, 40;** *2, 3, 60;* 13, 31, 33–34, 36, 110, 122, 140, 142, 150, 154 and see Goshawk and Sparrowhawk
Heron (grey) *Ardea cinerea* Linnaeus   **14, 30;** *6;* 14–16, 18, 90, 92, 118, 122
Heron, night *Nycticorax nycticorax* (Linnaeus)   42
Heron, white   **15**
Hobby *Falco subbuteo* Linnaeus   34
Hoopoe *Upupa epops* Linnaeus   **40;** *44;* 52, 53, 55, 136, 164, 170, 172
Hosgrinius   106
Hroc   57

Jackdaw *Corvus monedula* Linnaeus **29;** 56, 57, 77
Jay *Garrulus glandarius* (Linnaeus) **13A, 13B, 15, 24, 26, 27, 30, 40;** *21, 40;* 41, 57, 73, 75, 76, 78, 140, 144, 150, 154
Jay, blue *Cyanocitta cristata* (Linnaeus) 116

Kingfisher *Alcedo atthis* (Linnaeus)   **1, 2, 14, 15, 31;** 53–55, 68, 118, 120
Kite   **10, 40;** 33, 34
Kite, black *Milvus migrans* (Boddaert) 158
Kite, red *Milvus milvus* (Linnaeus)   158

Lammergeier *Gypaetus barbatus* (Linnaeus)   **40**
Lapwing *Vanellus vanellus* (Linnaeus) **10;** *43;* 52
Lark *Alauda arvensis* Linnaeus   *53;* 60, 68
Linnet *Acanthis cannabina* (Linnaeus) **29, 33, 46A;** 59–60, 75, 144

Magpie *Pica pica* (Linnaeus)   **10, 13A, 14, 15, 16, 19, 23, 24, 27, 28, 40;** *2, 21;* 37, 55, 57, 75, 92, 140, 144, 150
Mallard *Anas platyrhynchos* Linnaeus 22, 29; 31, 34, 144
Martin, house *Delichon urbica* (Linnaeus) **12A** (nest), **20;** 61, 112
Merlin *Falco columbarius* Linnaeus   34
Mew   47
Moorhen *Gallinula chloropus* (Linnaeus) 52
Mose cok, mose hen   150
Muskett   34

Nightingale *Luscinia megarhynchos* Brehm   64, 65, 100
Nuthatch *Sitta europea* Linnaeus   *54;* 68

Oriole, golden *Oriolus oriolus* (Linnaeus)   **39**
Ortolan *Emberiza hortulana* Linnaeus 60, 82
Osprey *Pandion haliaetus* (Linnaeus) 114
Ostrich *Struthio camelus* Linnaeus   55, 82, 150
Owl   **9, 10, 11B, 13A, 14, 16, 19, 27, 29, 45;** *12, 19, 20, 21, 22, 40, 54;* 19, 23, 35–42, 68, 75, 92, 110, 140, 144, 164, 172
Owl, barn *Tyto alba* (Scopoli)   39, 166
Owl, eagle *Bubo bubo* (Linnaeus)   39
Owl, little *Athene noctua* (Scopoli)   **39;** *59;* 36, 39, 76, 166
Owl, long-eared *Asio otus* (Linnaeus) **44;** *23;* 37, 39
Owl, short-eared *Asio flammeus* (Pontoppidan)   37
Owl, tawny *Strix aluco* Linnaeus **24, 26;** 36, 166

Parrakeet, rose-ringed *Psittacula krameri* (Scopoli)   *33;* 43
Parrot   **11B, 15, 17, 47;** *32, 33;* 12, 43, 57, 75, 92, 140, 144, 150, 164, 170
Partridge (grey) *Perdix perdix* (Linnaeus) **2, 40;** *15, 16;* 28–29, 31, 92, 108, 122 144
Partridge, chukar *Alectoris chukar* (Gray) 92
Partridge, red-legged *Alectoris rufa* (Linnaeus)   **2, 40;** *16;* 28

Peacock, peafowl, peahen *Pavo cristatus* Linnaeus   **6, 10, 11B, 19, 28, 38, 39, 44, 47;** *8, 9, 10, 59;* 19, 20, 23, 28, 35, 52, 73, 75, 76, 86, 88, 92, 108, 150, 156
Pelican   **41;** 59, 82, 116
Pelican, Dalmatian *Pelecanus crispus* Bruch   160
Pelican, White *Pelecanus onocratulus* Linnaeus   160
Peregrine see Falcon
Pheasant *Phasianus colchicus* Linnaeus **38, 40, 44;** 30–31, 92, 122, 150, 154, 170, 172
Pigeon   **2;** 44–46, 68
Pigeon, domestic see Dove
Pigeon, wood *Columba Palumbus* Linnaeus   **1;** 46, 92
Ptarmigan *Lagopus mutus* (Montin)   31
Quail *Coturnix coturnix* (Linnaeus) 28–29, 78, 118

Rail, water *Rallus aquaticus* Linnaeus **2;** 52
Raredumle   18
Raven *Corvus corax* Linnaeus   **8, 9, 14, 23, 28, 40;** 56, 57, 94
Redstart *Phoenicurus phoenicurus* (Linnaeus)   64, 65
Robin *Erithacus rubecula* (Linnaeus) **10, 11A, 24, 29, 30, 33, 42;** 59, 64, 65, 77, 150, 170, 172
Rook *Corvus frugilegus* Linnaeus   **19;** 56, 57, 71

Scealfer   48
Shelduck *Tadorna tadorna* (Linnaeus) 31
Shoveler *Annas clypeata* (Linnaeus)   16, 31
Shrike   69
Shrike, great grey *Lanius excubitor* Linnaeus   **37A;** 68, 69
Shrike, lesser grey *Lanius minor* Gmelin 152
Skylark *Alauda arvensis* Linnaeus   *53;* 68
Smew *Mergus albellus* Linnaeus   31
Snipe *Gallinago gallinago* (Linnaeus) *41;* 50

INDEX OF BIRDS

Sparrow   30, 60, 102
Sparrow, hedge *Prunella modularis* (Linnaeus)   **1**; 70
Sparrow, house *Passer domesticus* (Linnaeus)   **2, 14**; 60, 140
Sparrowhawk *Accipiter nisus* (Linnaeus)   **24, 29**; 33, 34, 160, 170
Spoonbill *Platalea leucorodia* Linnaeus   **30**; 15–16, 18, 49
Starling *Sturnus vulgaris* Linnaeus   **34B**; 70
Stonechat *Saxicola torquata* (Linnaeus)   64, 144
Stork   *4, 7;* 14–15, 92, 116, 118, 144, 164
Stork, black *Ciconia nigra* (Linnaeus)   15, 108
Stork, white *Ciconia ciconia* (Linnaeus)   **14, 19, 40;** *5;* 14, 15, 18, 56, 140, 150
Swallow (barn) *Hirundo rustica* Linnaeus   **10, 12A, 17, 42, 43;** *47, 48, 49;* 51, 61–62, 75, 92
Swallow, red-rumped *Hirundo daurica* Linnaeus   **12B** (nest)
Swan (mute) *Cygnus olor* (Gmelin)   **8, 9, 10, 14, 19, 28;** *2, 11, 12;* 24–25, 94, 108, 140, 144, 154
Swifts Apodidae   61

Tarin   60
Teal *Anas crecca* Linnaeus   **48A;** 31
Thrush   64–65, 78
Thrush, mistle *Turdus viscivorus* Linnaeus   64
Thrush, song *Turdus philomelos* Brehm   **1, 10, 48C;** 64, 65, 142, 144
Tit   66–67
Tit, blue *Parus caeruleus* Linnaeus   **27, 35A;** *21;* 66, 140, 142, 150, 164
Tit, coal *Parus ater* Linnaeus   **25;** 58, 66, 67
Tit, great *Parus major* Linnaeus   **35B, 41, 43, 46B;** *56;* 52, 58, 66, 75, 76, 78, 140
Tit, long-tailed *Aegithalos caudatus* (Linnaeus)   *52;* 66, 67

Vulture   **40;** 27, 114, 164

Wagster   70
Wagtail   30, 70
Wagtail, pied *Motacilla alba* Linnaeus   **48B;** 70
Warbler (including *Phylloscopus*)   70
Waryghanger   152
Wealhafoc   34
Weirangle   152
Wheatear *Oenanthe oenanthe* (Linnaeus)   144
Woodcock *Scolopax rusticola* Linnaeus   **15, 33;** *40;* 50, 51, 96, 108
Woodpecker   54–55
Woodpecker, great spotted *Dendrocopus major* (Linnaeus)   **42;** 54, 55, 78
Woodpecker, green *Picus viridis* Linnaeus   **1, 14, 25, 47;** 54, 78, 128, 144, 150, 170
Woodpecker, lesser spotted *Dendrocopus minor* (Linnaeus)   55, 162
Wórhana   31
Wren *Troglodytes troglodytes* (Linnaeus)   **11A, 15, 28, 43, 44, 47;** *2;* 70, 126, 140, 144, 150

Yellowhammer *Emberiza citrinella* Linnaeus   60

B. Bestiary birds

Accipiter   33, 34, 106
Alcion   54
Alauda   70
Alietus   34
Anas   24
Anser   23, 106
Aquila   **18A;** 27, 106
Ardea   16–18, 106
Assida   *45;* 55, 82

Bernace   49
Bubo   39, 42
Bucio, butio   18

Capus   34
Carduelis   60
Ciconia, cyconia   **20A;** *7;* 16, 18, 106
Columba   46

Corax   57
Cornix   57
Corvus   22, 56, 57, 106
Coturnix   30
Cuculus   53
Cygnus   25, 105

Falco   33, 70
Fenix   **19;** 10, 82

Gallina, gallus   20
Graculus   57, 75
Grus   16, 18, 116

(H)irundo, hyrurdo   **17A, 17B;** 61–62

Luscinia   65

Martinetas   **20A, 20B;** 54, 68
Mergulus, mergus   49
Merula   55
Mesange   67
Milvus   34
Monedula   57

Noctua   **19;** *24, 25, 26, 27;* 39, 42
Nycticorax   *28, 29, 30, 31;* 42

Olor   25
(H)onocratulus   18, 22

Passer   50, 106
Pavo   20, 23
Pelicanus   **11A, 19;** 49, 82, 160
Perdix   29–30
Phoenix = fenix
Pica   55, 104
Picus   54, 55, 104
Psitacus   43

Regulus   70

Struthio = assida

Turdus   65
Turtur   46

Upupa   52, 53

Vultur   **18B;** 27

INDEX OF MANUSCRIPTS

Alnwick Castle, H.G. The Duke of Northumberland
  Transitional Bestiary   18, 35
  The Sherborne Missal   **36, 37;** *6, 18, 38, 39, 41, 52, 53;* 15, 28, 30, 31, 32, 47, 50, 53, 54, 59, 60, 64, 68, 70, 82, 174

Avesnes, Société Archéologique
  Detached Bible leaf   26

Bergamo, Biblioteca Communale
  Delta vii.14 Sketchbook of Giovaninno de Grassi   52, 82, 158

Brussels, Bibliothèque Royale
  9961–9962 Peterborough Psalter   **29, 30;** 15, 53, 56, 76
  11060–11061 The Brussels Hours of John Duke of Berry   66

Cambridge, University Library
  Dd.1.14 Bible   66
  Dd.4.17 Hours of Alice de Reydon   34
  Dd.8.2 Miscellaneous   37, 45
  Dd.12.67 Psalter   122, 154
  Ee.3.59 History of St. Edward   49
  Ee.4.37 Sir Peter Idley's Instructions   **39**
  Gg.6.5 'Fourth family' Bestiary   11, 34, 53
  Ii.4.26 'Second family' Bestiary   11
  Kk.4.25 'Third family' Bestiary   34, 49, 53, 62, 70
  Mm.5.31 Apocalypse of Alexander of Bremen   **14;** 54, 60
  Add.4082 The Montacute Psalter   16
  Add.4083 Bible of Philip the Fair   39
  Add.4085 Psalter   51
  Add.6159 Bible   *49*

Cambridge, Fitzwilliam Museum
  12 Psalter   22
  20 Bestiary of William the Norman (Guillaume le Clerc)   53
  242 The Grey-FitzPayn Hours   **32;** 59, 66, 138
  254 'Third family' Bestiary   53, 57, 70
  298 The Metz Pontifical (Breviary of Margaret de Bar)   20, 132, 140
  379 'Second family' Bestiary   18, 52, 60
  2–1954 The Bird Psalter   **33, 48A, 48B;** 15, 23, 24, 28, 31, 47, 50, 53, 54, 56, 59, 64, 65, 70
  McLean 15 Bible   *5;* 15, 47, 66
  McLean 123 Bestiary of William the Norman (Guillaume le Clerc)   46
  The Pilkington Charter   29, 36

Cambridge, Christ's College
  8 Book of Hours   53

Cambridge, Corpus Christi College
  16 Matthew Paris, Chronica Majora   60
  48 Bible   23
  53 Psalter and 'Second family' Bestiary   24, 52, 76

Cambridge, Emmanuel College
  112 Gregory, Moralia   **48D;** 64, 70

Cambridge, Gonville and Caius College
  361/442 Bible   36

Cambridge, Magdalene College, Pepysian Library
  1916 Sketchbook   **2;** *10, 16;* 15, 16, 23, 28, 31, 49, 50, 52, 53, 58, 60, 64, 68, 75, 76

Cambridge, Sidney Sussex College
  Delta 3.17 (James 62) Diurnale   69
  Delta 5.11 (James 96) Bible   **12A**
  Delta 5.15 (James 100) Bestiary (Aviarium)   *7, 29;* 18, 25

Cambridge, Trinity College
  B.5.3 (James 149) Gospels   36
  B.10.4 (James 215) Gospels   *9;* 20, 35
  B.11.4 (James 243) Psalter   *45*
  B.11.22 (James 261) Book of Hours   **31;** 15, 51, 54, 58, 66, 70, 74
  O.1.57 (James 1081) Miscellaneous   37
  O.1.14 (James 1118) Bestiary of William the Norman (Guillaume le Clerc)   *31*
  O.4.27 (James 1258) Bible   *48*
  R.4.12 (James 645) Chronicles   36
  R.16.2 (James 950) Apocalypse   **13A & B;** 19, 24, 28, 71, 73, 108
  R.17.7 (James 993) Abingdon Chronicle   *42;* 52

Cambridge, Trinity Hall
  12 Le Roman de Chastelaine de Vergi etc   60

Cambridge, Massachusetts, Hofer Collection
  Hofer-Kraus Bestiary (Aviarium)   65, 76

Chantilly, Musée Condé
  1284 Les Très Riches Heures of John Duke of Berry   56, 66, 132
  Hours of Etienne Chevalier   170

Douai, Municipal Library
  171 Psalter   134

Dublin, Trinity College

INDEX OF MANUSCRIPTS

A.I.6 Gospels (Book of Kells) **5;** *13, 14;* 19, 20, 26, 71, 92
Durham, Dean and Chapter Library
  B.II.8 St. Jerome, Commentary on Isaiah 35

Eton College
  177 Apocalypse 46

Florence, Biblioteca Laurenziana
  Plut.1.56 Rabula Gospels 31, 92
Florence, Biblioteca Nazionale
  L.F.22 Hours of Giangaleazzo Visconti 34

Glasgow, University Library
  U.3.2. (Hunter 229) Psalter 15, 22
  U.4.9 (Hunter 251) John Arderne, Practice of Chirurgerie 70
  U.5.9 (Hunter 269) Guillaume Tardiff, Livre de l'Art de Fauconnerie, Venerie et la Chasse 28, 122
  U.8.7 (Hunter 339) John Arderne, Opera 70

Hereford, Cathedral Library
  P.7.v Digestum **48C**

Leningrad, Public Library
  Qu.v.1 Transitional Bestiary 35
London, British Library
  Add.10546 Moûtier-Grandval Bible 55
  Add.11283 'Second family' Bestiary 24
  Add.11695 Beatus, Commentary on the Apocalypse *1*
  Add.16997 Hours of Etienne Chevalier **44, 45, 46;** *23;* 39, 46, 60
  Add.17333 Apocalypse 58
  Add.24686 Alphonso (Tennison) Psalter **1, 21, 22, 23;** *17, 31, 37, 46, 51;* 54, 64, 65, 76, 78
  Add.27695 Cocharelli, Tractatus de Vitis Septem **41;** 49
  Add.28841 Cocharelli, Tractatus de Vitis Septem 158
  Add.29301 John Arderne, Medical Works 70
Add.29433 Book of Hours 55, 70
Add.35311 Breviary of John the Fearless 16
Add.36684 St. Omer Hours 58
Add.39810 St. Omer Psalter **28;** *2;* 23, 46, 56, 136
Add.42130 Luttrell Psalter **34;** *22, 33;* 30, 37, 53, 56, 70
Add.42555 Abingdon Apocalypse *20;* 36
Add.47682 The Holkham Bible Picture Book **10, 11, 12;** 34, 49, 52, 56, 61, 64, 160
Add.49999 Book of Hours *19;* 36
Add.54180 La Somme le Roi *56;* 66
Arundel 83 De Lisle (Arundel) Psalter **27;** *21;* 66, 136
Arundel 157 Psalter 22
Burney 3 Bible of Robert de Bello **9;** *12;* 19, 24, 35, 46, 56
Cotton Claudius B IV Aelfric's Metrical Paraphrase of the Pentateuch and Joshua **8;** 19, 24, 56
Cotton Julius A.VI Hymnal *3;* 13, 34
Cotton Nero D.IV Lindisfarne Gospels **3, 4;** *8;* 20, 26, 71, 92
Cotton Tiberius B.V Marvels of the East 13
Cotton Tiberius C.VI Psalter *34, 35;* 45
Cotton Vespasian A.I Psalter 19
Egerton 613 Bestiary of William the Norman (Guillaume le Clerc) 30, 46
Egerton 1070 London Hours of René of Anjou **47;** 54
Egerton 3127 Cocharelli, Tractatus de Vitis Septem **40;** *44;* 28, 53, 158
Egerton 3781 Cocharelli, Tractatus de Vitis Septem 158
Harley 273 Bestiaire d'amours 18, 25, 65
Harley 603 Copy of Utrecht Psalter *11;* 23, 24
Harley 2449 Miscellaneous Prayers etc. 66
Harley 2788 Golden Gospels **6;** 20
Harley 2795 Gospels 20
Harley 2821 Echternach Gospels **7**
Harley 2887 Book of Hours *59;* 23, 156
Harley 3244 'Second family' Bestiary *27;* 35
Harley 4751 'Second family' Bestiary **17A; 20B;** *25;* 18, 23, 46, 49, 73
Harley 6563 Book of Hours 122
Harley 7026 Lovell Lectionary **38**
Royal 1B.xii Bible of William of Hales 36
Royal 1D.i Bible of William of Devon *32, 47;* 12, 43, 74, 76, 102
Royal 1D.x Psalter 19
Royal 1E.vii Bible *36;* 27, 45
Royal 1E.ix Bible of Richard II *50;* 154
Royal 2B.vii Queen Mary's Psalter *15;* 18, 28, 122
Royal 3D.vi Petrus Comestor, Historia Scholastica (Ashridge College) **35A;** 60, 66
Royal 10E.iv Smithfield Decretals **35B;** 20, 30, 36, 66
Royal 12C.xix Transitional Bestiary **18;** *28;* 27, 34
Royal 13B.viii Giraldus Cambrensis, Opera **20A;** 64
Royal 14C.vii Matthew Paris, Chronica Majora & Historia Anglorum *4;* 14
Royal 15D.ii Apocalypse 26
Royal 15E.iii Bartholomew Glanvill, Le Livre des Proprietez des Choses **19;** 15, 160
Royal 19B.xv Apocalypse with figures **15;** 15, 50, 110
Royal 20D.iv Lancelot du Lac *43;* 52
Sloane 278 Bestiary (Aviarium) 65
Sloane 3544 'Second family' Bestiary 62, 65
Stowe 17 Maestricht Horae 54
Yates Thompson 8 Verdun Breviary (first part) 140
London, Lambeth Palace
  3 Lambeth Bible 22
  75 Apocalypse 26, 36, 37, 46, 76
  89 Bible 76
  186 Psalter 156
  209 Apocalypse *54;* 46, 68

233 Bardolf-Vaux Psalter 66, 70
London, Royal College of Physicians,
  Wilton Psalter 20, 23
London, Victoria and Albert Museum
  1346/1891 Missal of St. Denys **43**;
    61, 66, 74
  Salting 1222 Hours of Marguerite de
    Foix 58, 69
London, Westminster Abbey Library
  22 'Third family' Bestiary 49, 55, 60,
    65, 70
Longleat House, The Marquess of Bath
  Longleat Psalter 34
Los Angeles, Gulbenkian Collection
  134 (formerly Yates Thompson 55)
    Apocalypse 19

Manchester, John Rylands University
Library
  Latin 10 Gospels 23
  Latin 19 Apocalypse *58;* 73, 110
  Latin 164 Book of Hours 52, 54, 60

New Haven, Yale University, Beineke
Library
  404 The Rothschild Canticles 61
New York, Pierpont Morgan Library
  102 Windmill Psalter 30
  302 Ramsey Psalter (part) 76
  524 Apocalypse 110
New York Metropolitan Museum of Art,
Cloisters Collection
  Prayer-book of Bonne of Luxembourg
    39, 52, 70

Oxford, Bodleian Library
  Ashmole 1511 'Second family'
    Bestiary 18, 23, 62
  Ashmole 1523 The Bromholm Psalter
    16
  Auctarium D.1.17 Bible **12B**; 14

Auctarium D.4.17 Apocalypse *57;*
  73, 110
Bodley 264 Romance of Alexander
  29, 53, 54, 58, 61
Bodley 283 Mirroure of the World
  156
Bodley 602i Bestiary (Aviarium) 34
Bodley 764 'Second family' Bestiary
  17B; 18, 23, 34, 49, 61
Bodley 912 Bestiary of William the
  Norman (Guillaume le Clerc) 46
Douce 35 Statutes of England 36
Douce 88ii 'Third family' Bestiary
  18, 23, 52, 65, 70
Douce 93 Hours of Yolande de Lalaing
  14
Douce 151 'Second family' Bestiary
  26, 30; 18, 23
Douce 180 Apocalypse 19, 78
Douce 219/220 Hours of Engelbert of
  Nassau 20, 73
Douce 366 The Ormesby Psalter **24,
  25, 26**; 36, 59, 70, 136, 174
Junius 11 Anglo-Saxon versions of
  parts of Genesis etc (the Caedmon
  Manuscript) 20
e Musaeo 60 Boniface VIII Sext. 36
e Musaeo 136 'Third family' Bestiary
  70
Rawlinson Poetry 223 Lydgate, The
  Siege of Troy (Fragment) 37, 186
Oxford, All Souls College
  6 Amesbury Psalter 23
Oxford, Lincoln College
  16 Apocalypse *40;* 73, 110
Oxford, New College
  65 Apocalypse **16**; 47
Oxford, St. John's College
  61 'Second family' Bestiary 35
  178 'Second family' Bestiary 35, 58
Oxford, University College

165 Bede, Life of St. Cuthbert 56, 71
Paris, Bibliothèque Nationale
  fr.403 Apocalypse 110
  fr.1586 Guillaume de Machaut, Le
    Remède de Fortune 164
  fr.19093 Sketchbook of Villard de
    Honnecourt 25
  lat.919 Les Grandes Heures of John
    Duke of Berry 61, 66
  lat.3093 Les Très Belles Heures de
    Notre Dame of John Duke of Berry
    39
  lat.9471 The Rohan Book of Hours
    29, 57, 66
  lat.10483/10484 The Belleville Breviary
    30–31
  lat 18014 Les Petites Heures of John
    Duke of Berry 66
  nouv.acq.lat. 3145 The Hours of
    Jeanne de Navarre **42**; 61
Rome, Vatican Library
  Pal.Lat. 1071 Emperor Frederick II,
    De Arte Venandi cum Avibus 9, 28,
    33, 49, 55, 56, 122, 160, 166
  Lat. 5729 Forfar Bible 29

Utrecht, Bibiotheek der Rijksuniversiteit
  Script.eccl.484 Utrecht Psalter 23

Venice, Library of the Mechitarist
Fathers
  196 Gospels 31
Verdun, Public Library
  107 Verdun Breviary (second part)
    140
Vienna, Österreichische
Nationalbibliothek
  338 Golden Bull of the Emperor
    Wenceslas 52
  1856 Black Hours of Charles the Rash
    Duke of Burgundy 46

GENERAL INDEX

Aachen 90
Ada 90
Adam naming animals 19, 35, 58, 94
Aesop 140
Alexander, J. J. G. 30, 164
Alexander Neckam 23
Alexander of Bremen 106
Annunciation 44
Apocalypse 8, 9, 13, 19, 26, 35, 57, 73, 76, 104, 110
Aristotle 39, 43, 54, 64, 65
Ark 19, 20, 46, 56, 94, 96, 98
Ashridge College 148
Aviaries 75, 170
Aviarium 11, 18, 20, 23, 25, 34, 55, 57, 58, 61, 65
Avril, F. 162, 164

Baptism 44
Bartholomew Anglicus or Glanvill 15
Barton 53
Berry, John Duke of 66, 166, 168
Bestiary 8, 9, 10–11, 75
Bibles 8, 9, 35, 96
Bird-catching **27;** *21;* 156
Boke of St. Albans 33
Boucicault Master 166, 172
Brieger, P. H. 104
Brown, G. Baldwin 86
Bruce-Mitford, R. L. S. 84, 86
Butterfly **24**

Cage-birds 57, 58, 65, 75, 104
Call of the Birds **13, 14, 15, 16;** *1, 57, 58;* 9, 35, 54, 56, 104, 106, 108, 110
Canon tables **7;** *9, 13;* 20, 23, 26, 31, 92

Canterbury 94, 96, 98
Caricatured birds 58
Cecchelli et al. 92
Charlemagne 90
Clarke, W. Eagle 86
Copying 73–74
Creation **8, 9, 10;** *12;* 13, 15, 19, 24, 35, 44, 56, 94, 96, 98
Cybo d'Hyères 158

Deer **21, 27, 28, 29**
Dodwell, C. R. 26
Drawing 73–76
Drolleries **21, 24, 26, 29;** 36, 124, 130, 140

East Anglian manuscripts 70, 78, 98, 120, 126, 132, 134, 136, 138, 144, 146, 148, 174
Echternach 92
Egerton Master 172
Evangelists 26
Evans, A. H. 108
Ezekiel 26

Fall of Babylon 104
Fenland manuscripts 136
Flowers 128

Gervaise 11
Giotto 78
Giraldus Cambrensis 49, 54, 64, 68, 118
Gospels 8
Gothic period 71
Great Gransden 53
Guillaume le Clerc *31;* 11

Hassall, W. O. 98, 100
Hawking *3;* 28, 33, 34, 122
Henry, F. 88
Hours, Books of 8, 9, 19, 23, 24, 25, 31, 36, 54, 58, 66, 70
Howe, W. N. 73
Hugh of Folieto 11
Hunting **29, 32;** 138
Hutchinson, G. E. 31, 43, 60, 120, 142

Isidore of Seville 11
Ives, S. A. and Lehmann-Haupt, H. 76

James, M. R. 10, 22, 82, 104, 106, 140
Jean Le Noir 162
Jesse 100

Kendrick, T. D. et al. 84
Klingender, F. 106

Labours of the Months 13, 24
Ladybird **24**
Loisel, G. 172
London 98, 120, 148
Longnon, J. and Cazelles, R. 132

McCulloch, F. 10, 55, 67, 70
Macdonald 86
Martindale, A. 78
Marvels of the East 13
Matthew Paris 14
Meiss, M. 166, 172
Model-books 75–76
Monkey **21, 26, 29;** *20*

Pächt, O. 78, 82, 158
Pentecost 44, 45

Philippe de Thaon   11
Physiologus   10
Pierre de Beauvais   11, 18, 25, 65, 67
Presentation in the Temple   46
Psalters   8, 9, 19, 22, 36, 57

Ray, J.   39, 124, 132
Remède de Fortune, Artist of   164
Revelation, Book of   8
Reynard the Fox   **29**; 20, 23, 24, 37
Ripley, Dillon   43
Romanesque period   71

St. Francis   13, 16, 36, 106
St. John   19, 26, 84, 88
St. Kevin   64
St. Peter   19
Sandler, L. F.   76, 128, 136, 138

Scheller, R. W.   76, 82
Scott, K. A.   156
Sherborne Abbey   150
Smithfield Priory   148
Snail   **24**
Spain   9
Squirrel   **24**; *54*
Sutton Hoo Treasure   *60;* 122
Sweet, H.   14, 20, 23, 31
Syferwas (Siferwas), John   148, 150, 152
Symbolism, symbols   13, 22, 26, 27, 35, 36, 44, 45, 46, 84

Ticehurst, N. F.   24
Tobit   **12;** *47, 48, 49, 50;* 61, 102, 154
Tree of Knowledge   100
Trèves   90

Trier   90
Tristram, H. B.   94
Turner, William   108

Unicorn   **25;** 128

Vaurie, C.   38, 70

Watts, G. F.   84
Webster, J. C.   34
White, T. H.   11, 42
William the Norman   11, 30, 45, 53
Winchcombe   144
Wright, T.   31, 100

Yapp, W. B.   33, 76, 82

Zephaniah   22